Winning the Job Search

The Hard Truths about Getting Hired

Anthony Garone and Ellis Fitch
Edify Content

Winning the Job Search: The Hard Truths about Getting Hired

Other books by Anthony Garone

Clueless at The Work: Advice from a Corporate Tyrant
Failure to Fracture: Learning King Crimson's Impossible Song

Also by Ellis Fitch (as Ellis Friedman)

A Valediction

Visit Anthony online at http://garone.org/
Visit Edify Content at https://edifycontent.com/

Cover design by Guy Corp, www.GrafixCorp.com

STAIRWAY≡PRESS

STAIRWAY PRESS—APACHE JUNCTION

www.stairwaypress.com
1000 West Apache Trail, Suite 126
Apache Junction, AZ 85120 USA

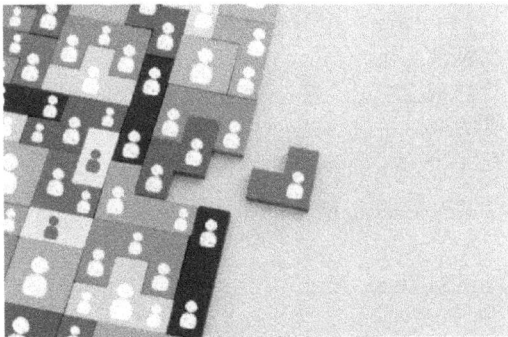

Thanks

ANTHONY AND ELLIS are especially grateful to the people who volunteered their time and energy to contribute their expertise in this book:

- Jamie Contino
- Allen Plunkett
- Tracy Olnhausen
- Marquess Lewis
- Carmen West
- Jeremy Wilson
- Vita Duncan

Many of them have websites and are happy to connect on LinkedIn. Check 'em out.

Anthony would like to thank:

- Sarah Garone for her loving me for who I am and always encouraging me to be better.
- Ellis Fitch for her excellent contributions to this book and being a great writing partner who rightly challenges my perspective.
- All the hiring managers and company owners who invested in me, especially Dave Woodruff, Mike

Moulton, Justin Grossman, Marty Birecki, Jim McCarthy, Steve Vai, Chuck Rossi, Marquess Lewis, Danny Hillis, Brad Patten, Bill Gau, Rudy Bellavia, Ed Stolze, Jim Bogner, Steve Gobbell, Cory Berg, and Anila Arthanari.

- Ken Coffman, my partner in so many crimes.

Ellis would like to thank:

- James Fitch for being unendingly supportive and loving.
- My mom Lisa Sorg-Friedman for her corporate anecdotes, using her network to get me jobs, and being an all-around badass.
- Anthony Garone for engaging with my unending challenges to his perspective.
- The amazing leaders and mentors I've worked with, namely Carey Ballard, Amanda Seider, and Johna Burke.

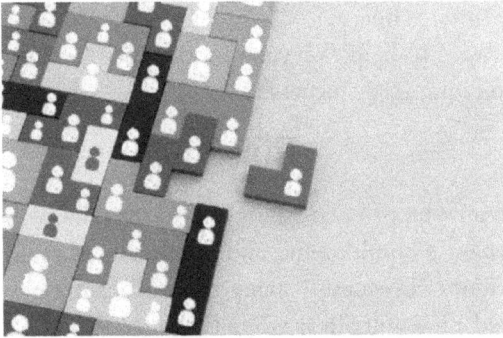

Introduction

Background

YOU'RE NOT GONNA take advice from a coupla nobodies, so allow us to introduce ourselves before we get started.

Anthony Garone

I am an entrepreneur and hiring manager with blah-blah-blah and years of experience. Average-sized man. Hired a zillion people, fired a few. Reviewed thousands of resumes. Helped many friends and family find new jobs and even find new careers by changing industries. Advised several startups and university/community college programs. 20 years in IT and software, a couple of failed startups, founder of a growing international YouTube channel called Make Weird Music.[1] Author of *Clueless at The Work: Advice from a Corporate Tyrant*[2] and *Failure to Fracture: Learning King Crimson's Impossible Song.*[3]

More importantly, in 2020 I had more people than ever reach out to me asking to help find a job. Whether it's for themselves or for their spouse or family member, it doesn't matter. There are a lot of people looking for jobs and the

---

[1] https://youtube.com/makeweirdmusic

[2] https://www.amazon.com/Clueless-Work-Advice-Corporate-Tyrant/dp/1949267296

[3] https://failuretofracture.com/

competition is fierce.

I want to help everyone I can to find gainful employment and find long-term success.

Ellis Fitch

A woman who pretends she's bought into the corporate world. 10+ years of multimedia and content marketing experience. Many ignored resumes, many successful interviews. I've even declined a few job offers when I wasn't looking.

I've gone through the job hunt a few times, and each time, it's just as dehumanizing. Especially during COVID, the deck was stacked against job hunters. But that doesn't mean you can't do anything about it! We're showing you in this book how to take as much control of getting hired and growing your career as possible. We hope you use this book to empower yourself, your resume, and your career.

Our Expert Contributors

To provide you with a diverse background of insights, we recruited several experts from our network to provide feedback, anecdotes, counterpoints, and other information you will find useful.

- Jamie Contino, External Recruiter, Prosum
- Tracy Olnhausen, Internal Department Leader
- Allen Plunkett, CEO and External Recruiter, Phoenix Staff
- Marquess Lewis, CTO and Sales Executive
- Jeremy Wilson, CTO and Serial Entrepreneur
- Vita Duncan, PHR, SHRM-CP, sHRBP, HR operations leader
- Carmen West, Senior global HR leader and consultant

Context

We began writing this book in October 2020, about seven months into the COVID pandemic in the U.S. The numbers varied depending on who was reporting, but it's safe to say that at least 20 million Americans lost their jobs in 2020. And who knows how many people had their jobs affected by reduced pay, reduced hours, furloughs, and other situations.

The market was flooded with candidates looking for employment. We personally knew a few dozen people who were unemployed and unable to find work. Most of these people are talented, smart, and some come from in-demand roles.

When we talked to them about finding a new job, they felt stuck. They felt hopeless. They saw no light at the end of the tunnel.

It was terrible.

So we wrote this guide to get straight to the most valuable and helpful information for our friends, family, former colleagues, and you to find work, even if the worst of the COVID economy has passed (knock wood). There's some tough advice in here, and maybe some stuff you'll disagree with, but for some people, any advice is better than no advice.

The book is built on a series of misconceptions we've seen exhibited by both employed and unemployed people. We all have false beliefs about getting hired.

We finished writing the book about a year later, in September 2021. The COVID pandemic appears to be ending (as of April 2022) and we're in this awkward transition stage of will-this-thing-ever-end? There are remnants throughout this book of being deep into the pandemic. We did what we could to edit out signs of those particular times, but some of it still made it to print. Though a lot of the commentary is applicable in the long-term, you'll have to forgive our COVID tunnel-vision, which I think every American had. Hopefully you'll see past it, pick up some new perspective, and go get a new job.

No matter what, we wish you luck, good health, and

wellness in finding your next position. We are all in this together!

What to Expect

This book is as straightforward and simple as possible. We are going to talk through nearly 60 hard truths and misconceptions that we see all the time with job applicants, unemployed folks, and people early in their careers. If you're looking for a job (during a pandemic or not), this book is for you.

Each misconception follows a simple template:

- The misconception
- A description of the misconception
- An anecdote or two
- Advice and commentary from our experts
- Commentary from Ellis
- What to do about the misconception
- Examples
- Key takeaways

In the "What to Do" sections, we provide meaningful advice that is clear and easy to follow. This advice is supplemented by insights from other professionals in our network. These professionals are business owners, recruiters, and hiring managers we've known for several years who have hired hundreds, if not thousands of people. Our recruiter friends have worked with tens of thousands of job-seekers and have literally reviewed hundreds of thousands of resumes.

The "What to Do" advice is the real deal. This book isn't some collection of anecdotal, single-point-of-view observations as you'll often find on the internet. Anthony has 20 years of experience across multiple industries, has interviewed hundreds of people, and hired (directly or leading the hiring committee) hundreds of people in the last 12 years.

While you might only spend a few minutes reading through each section, give yourself some time to ruminate on whether you've held the misconception, and what you're going to do about it. It's very difficult to unlearn a habitual perspective. Expect to be challenged and to grow a lot reading and working through this book.

The misconceptions in this book are not in any particular order. We tried to write about the most prevalent ones first. You may need misconception #42 way more than misconception #3.

Dig through and see what hits you.

What to Expect

This book served as a fun, collaborative writing project for me and Ellis that kicked off a long-term partnership. We started a business together through the process of writing this book and we're still at it. Our business is flourishing, and you can hire us to write for you.

Learn more about what we do at EdifyContent.com.

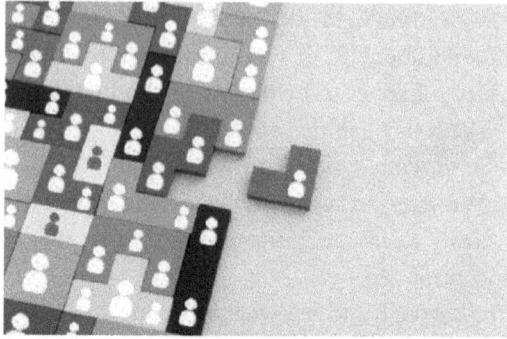

Preface

DOES THIS SOUND familiar?

You apply for positions and never hear back. You feel good about your resume, but get no bites. You might get an interview (or two) and then it's radio silence. Maybe you even get to salary negotiations, but everything falls apart. Or you end up with a disappointing offer that doesn't meet your expectations.

What's the deal?

In our experience, the problem is nearly universal: your perspective on what it means to get a job is naïve, or too centered on you.

We live in a world where everything's a click away. Orders from Amazon show up the next day at your doorstep. You sign petitions to make a difference in the world and you're not even wearing pants. You need a ride to the airport and it's there with a few finger-taps.

Simple! Quick! Cheap!

Why should getting a job be any different?

We've all seen the "Easy Apply" button on LinkedIn. One click and you're an applicant. LinkedIn even tells you, "Be one of the first 25 applicants." It makes you feel like you've done something to apply for that position, especially when you've clicked "Easy Apply" for 10 different roles today. And since you're one of the first applicants, you're going to be at the top of the pile!

We hate to break it to you, but it's all a lie. LinkedIn wants you to apply because getting more job applicants helps justify the hefty job advertising fees they levy against employers.

Job applications aren't a click-to-order process where step 1 leads to step 2, which leads to employment. The paradigm feels the same, so it's psychologically misleading. Applying for a job is sort of like a sale, except you're not buying a job. You're actually selling an employer on the idea that you are the perfect fit for their role. It's like ordering on Amazon, except the employer is the customer.

Let us explain...

A job gets posted because a company needs help and they (hopefully) have enough money to pay for that help. Once the job is posted, they can only hope their position is marketed well enough to reach the right people. Sometimes, they'll put thousands of dollars into promoting the role or they'll post it to their website and rely on word of mouth.

It's like casting a net in the ocean.

Sometimes the employer catches three applicants, sometimes they catch 300. Sometimes they pick up stuff they don't need (bots, unqualified applicants, people who don't live in the right geographies, etc.). Either way, the employer is looking for the best possible applicant given their own constraints. How big is their net? How many times do they want to cast the net? How long do they want to be out on the water? Is the net big enough for the fish they want to catch?

It's a game of timing, luck, and skill for both the employer and applicant. The employer has to cast the right size net in the best location to find the applicants they're looking for. It's much less deterministic than you might believe. You've likely only experienced it from the perspective of the job applicant, so we're hoping this book can help you see the perspective of the employer so you get a rare advantage.

If you're having a hard time getting a job, you want to make sure you're the most attractive prospect for the employer. The best way to do that is to frame your entire job application to meet the employer's expectations.

Terminology

Here are terms and abbreviations to understand before getting started:

- Cover letter: a formal introductory letter wherein you express your desire to get the job and demonstrate you have the skills and experience that align with what the employer has requested in the job description.
- Resume: a formal document that itemizes and illustrates your work history, significant career experiences, events and achievements. Also known as a Curriculum Vitae or CV.
- Job Description (JD): an internal- or external-advertisement through which a company expresses its desire to hire for a job.
- Job application: everything you submit (your resume, cover letter and other personal information) in response to a job description.
- Job applicant/candidate: the person who submits a job application.
- Internal recruiter: someone who acts on behalf of an employer to find applicants for a JD. This person is employed by the employer.
- External recruiter: someone who finds applicants for a JD, but does not work for the employer. An external recruiter is financially compensated by the employer when the applicant they referred is hired.
- Hiring manager: The person responsible for the job in question. This person generally writes the job description, looks at the resumes of the applicants, does most of the interviewing and handles the job offer, etc. If you get hired for the job, this person will be your boss.

Contents

Contents.. 1

Misconception #1: Unemployment is Your Fault............... 5

Misconception #2: The Job is for YOU........................... 7

Misconception #3: Your Resume Should Represent Your Work History 14

Misconception #4: The Job Description Actually Describes the Job... 21

Misconception #5: Your Resume stands Out, Therefore it will get Read... 26

Misconception #6: Hiring Managers Know How to Hire ... 35

Misconception #7: Internal Recruiters Know Who They're Looking For.. 39

Misconception #8: Your Work Speaks for Itself 44

Misconception #9: You Know How to Explain What You've Done.. 50

Misconception #10: All the Other Candidates are Telling the Truth.. 55

Misconception #11: You Must be Completely Honest 57

Misconception #12: Job Requirements are Requirements .. 61

Misconception #13: You Shouldn't Ask Your Friends to Help Get You an Interview at Their Company 67

Misconception #14: You Can't Prepare for an Interview ... 71

Misconception #15: You Can't Recreationally Interview ... 79

Misconception #16: LinkedIn is Stupid 82

Misconception #17: You Don't Need to Brag.................. 85

Misconception #18: Working Too Hard is a Weakness 88

Misconception #19: You Are as Good as You Think 91

Misconception #20: Your Personal Social Media Account Shouldn't Matter for Professional Stakes 94

Misconception #21: Your Appearance Doesn't Matter 98

Misconception #22: *You* are the Reason You Can't Get Hired 105

Misconception #23: Salary Website Data Will Get You More Money 108

Misconception #24: You're not Good Enough 120

Misconception #25: Your Resume Should Live on Your Hard Drive 127

Misconception #26: Using Introversion as an Excuse 130

Misconception #27: There Are No Jobs for You 137

Misconception #28: Your Skills are Timeless 143

Misconception #29: Short Answers are the Best 148

Misconception #30: It Shouldn't Be This Hard to Find a Job! 156

Misconception #31: The Best Time to Find a Job is When You Need One 160

Misconception #32: Everyone on the Hiring Team Will Vote to Hire You 163

Misconception #33: You Start a New Job with a Clean Slate 167

Misconception #34: Writing Isn't Important 171

Misconception #35: You Don't Need a Cover Letter 175

Misconception #36: External Recruiters Want You to Get Hired 180

Misconception #37: You're Joining a Family! 185

Misconception #38: You're too Old to Change Careers ... 190

Misconception #39: You Can Walk Into the Interview and Ace It 194

Misconception #40: Any Job is a Good Job 199

Misconception #41: One Resume to Rule Them All! 203

Misconception #42: It's Okay to talk about 2020 and 2021 207

Misconception #43: You Don't Like Your Job 211

Misconception #44: You Know What You Want in your Next Job 216

Misconception #45: There's Nothing you Can do to Stand Out 220

Misconception #46: Talking to a Recruiter is "an Offer" ... 226

Misconception #47: You Should Only Apply Once 230

Misconception #48: The Grass is Greener on the Other Side 234

Misconception #49: Sharing your Salary is Fine 238

Misconception #50: Your Current or Previous Employer Won't Find out About Your Interview 245

Misconception #51: You'll Never Meet the CEO, Anyway 249

Misconception #52: A Job is a Job is a Job 254

Misconception #53: You Don't Have to Learn about the Company Before You Interview 258

Misconception #54: You Can't Ask For Feedback 265

Misconception #55: You Can't Opt out of Ridiculous Interview Processes 271

3

Misconception #56: You Didn't Get the Job Because They Don't Like You 276

Quick Tips Before We Go 280

Conclusion 283

Misconception #57: The Best Job is Working for Someone Else 286

Additional Resources.. 289

Misconception #1: Unemployment is Your Fault

THERE'S A SOCIAL stigma for the unemployed. America has a very work-first mentality, and we tend to collectively classify our friends, family, and professional network peers as "unemployed" or "employed."

There's also this really perverse "hustle culture" all over social media. This stuff is the modern equivalent of the billboard and magazine cover supermodels we saw everywhere in the 1990s. You may have heard of concepts like body shaming. Hustle culture is the equivalent of employment shaming. It's just plain wrong.

Being unemployed can feel embarrassing.

So much of our daily conversation is, "What do you do for work?" It can be really awkward to say, "Oh, I'm unemployed right now."

You don't need to be embarrassed if you're unemployed.

Most of the people who lost their jobs during the COVID-19 epidemic suffered from a situation far beyond their control—and many haven't recovered. It wasn't an isolated incident where you were the problem and did something wrong that led to losing your job. I know software developers, aerospace engineers, and medical professionals who lost

5

employment. These are in-demand professions! They were supposedly recession-proof.

No one is immune from unemployment.

What we call *misconceptions* throughout this book are not reasons you're wrong and don't have a job. Instead, see them as a different way to think about the job search, and a different way to position yourself to prospective employers.

If you can't seem to get anywhere in your job search, maybe thinking differently will help you stand out from the crowd.

Don't blame yourself. As a hiring manager, I can tell you that people get jobs and lose jobs. I've seen the worst people get hired and I've seen the best people get into ruts.

COVID-19 was a two-year kidney punch; who knows what the rest of the decade will bring? Many studies show that we will see the economic impact of the global pandemic for years to come.

Regardless, don't let it win.

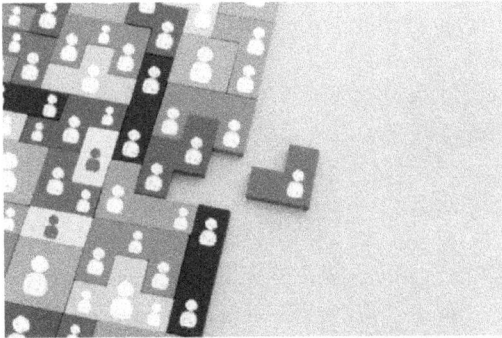

Misconception #2: The Job is for YOU

HOW MANY TIMES do you hear people say, "I found the perfect job!" Think about that sentiment. It's a me-first mentality. Being a job applicant is not a me-first situation. It's a please-hire-me situation. If your cover letter looks like this: "Dear Hiring Manager, This is the perfect job for me and here's why," all it shows is that you have no idea what you're talking about.

Hiring managers don't give a rodent's behind about whether the job is perfect for you. They're not trying to solve YOUR problem. They're hoping you can be the perfect person to solve THEIR problem.

Here's an anecdote from recruiter Allen Plunkett:

> As an employer, when I hear someone say, "It's like you wrote the job description with me in mind," there are few things [other than that] that set me in the immediate wrong direction with that person. It's so annoying. I 100% did not have you in mind, I didn't know you when I wrote it, I'm likely thinking that we won't even get along because you said it in the first place and now I don't want to hire you.

7

And another quick one-liner from HR leader Vita Duncan:

> *Hiring managers really do hate 'I feel like this job was made for me.'*

None of the above is meant to be heartless or insensitive, but rather to help you detach yourself emotionally from the job search process. One reason people suffer pain in the job search is they are too close to it. There's a lot of pressure we put on ourselves and there's the emotional and financial stress of not having any income. Considering the facts that 14% of Americans say they have wiped out their savings[1] and that most people didn't have much savings even before COVID,[2] being out of a job is brutal.

You will find a job. It may take a while. The economy will recover and change. You are adaptable. This is tough, and you can do this.

What to Do

Change your perspective and change your cover letter. Tell the hiring manager, "I feel like <u>I was made to do this job</u>!" YOU are the catch! You are the answer to all their problems! Stop sounding like the world revolves around you. It doesn't. And even if it does, don't tell your hiring manager.

Find ways to demonstrate *how* you are perfect for the job. In your cover letter, address the top three or four most important bullet points or sentences in the description. What I usually do is print out the job description, underline the

---

[1] https://www.cnbc.com/2020/09/01/nearly-14percent-of-americans-have-wiped-out-emergency-savings-during-pandemic.html
[2] https://www.axios.com/americans-emergency-savings-coronavirus-f11deffc-b8c1-48e0-a3db-0aeb3ce74fb9.html

important stuff, cross out the unimportant crap ("At Company, we are all about being the center of our customer's universe." *gag*), and find sentences that speak directly to your experience.

For example, "We are looking for a candidate that loves talking to customers." Okay. That's great. In your cover letter, you can say, "I love talking to customers! I have been in customer support for four years and have been recognized three times as a stand-out leader in my department."

Remember, you are the catch! Make the hiring manager feel like they'd regret not talking to the person who's gonna solve all their problems.

Example

Let's find some rando job description on LinkedIn and go through this exercise of finding what I like about a job and reframing it so it sounds like I'm a great fit for it.

Company Z ~~is recruiting for a~~ Director of Software Engineering. ~~This role would~~ report into the CTO ~~of the business~~.

~~The purpose of this role is to~~ build, lead and grow a world-class team of software developers and quality engineers who own the execution of the product feature development programme for all products/services within the product suite using solid engineering practices.

~~This role is~~ accountable for defining and executing on best practices, building high-performing teams, and the process necessary to have a scalable delivery model that uses both in house and external resources.

Key Responsibilities:
- Provide exceptional leadership to the engineering teams, optimising performance and continually

improving efficiency and capability

- Develop and implement a <u>robust technical engineering strategy that aligns with the needs of the business</u>
- <u>Establish best practice engineering and quality processes</u> to <u>reduce lead time</u> and <u>enhance quality/reliability</u> in conjunction with the Senior Technical Management team
- <u>Supervise, mentor and grow</u> members of the <u>local management and engineering team</u>
- <u>Collaborate</u> with architects, product managers and technical support to deliver high-quality, <u>technically sound products on schedule with great user experience</u>
- <u>Drive</u> all aspects of <u>recruiting</u> including, but not limited to, <u>attracting great talent and retaining</u> a highly-skilled, proficient engineering team
- Establish and maintain solid software engineering and quality management practices [They already mentioned this above!]

Required Skills:

- ~~Experience~~ delivering SaaS solutions
- ~~Extensive experience in~~ leading of Agile software development teams
- ~~Experience~~ designing, developing and delivering software ~~products~~
- ~~5+ years of~~ leading technical teams of 40+ ~~in a senior management position~~
- ~~Experience of~~ team transformation ~~to that of a~~ process-driven~~, scalable~~ high performing team
- ~~Experience of~~ transforming QA to an automated model

- ~~Excellent communication and organizational skills~~
- ~~Excellent interpersonal skills~~
- ~~Demonstrated creativity, problem-solving, and intelligent thinking~~
- ~~Excellent written English and verbal communication skills~~
- ~~Technologies~~ .NET/Kubernetes/Azure/Jira

I've struck through everything unimportant, assumed, or redundant. I've underlined everything I want to address in my job application.

Sentence One:

"Build, lead, and grow a world-class team of software developers and quality engineers who" blah-blah-blah. Okay, I will literally turn that sentence into, "I have built, led, and grown world-class teams of software developers and quality engineers who have" blah-blah-blah. I'll change some of the words around, of course, but otherwise I will largely mimic the language they use in the JD.

With regard to that last bit about "in-house and external resources", I'll add a sentence that says, "I have worked extensively with global teams across many time zones, whether they be in-house team members or external contractors."

Sentence Two:

"Accountable for defining and executing on best practices" blah-blah-blah.

I really enjoy doing this kind of work, so I could easily say, "I have been looking for a job where I can define and execute on best practices," which would make it sound like, "I'm looking for a great job and I think you're it!"

Or I could turn it around and say, "In my last two roles,

11

my companies have counted on me to define and execute on technical best practices. Doing so, I was able to blah-blah-blah." Here's where I am selling myself.

Key Responsibilities:

"Leadership to the engineering teams." "Robust technical and engineering practices." This is generally par for the course, so I find ways to sell my previous accomplishments that align with what they're seeking. And, again, I ensure that I don't make it sound like, "This is the perfect opportunity for me." Rather, "This is the obvious next step for you and for me."

I Might Write:

"My leadership skills have grown significantly in the past twelve years by managing cross-functional teams of various sizes across multiple continents." I want to sound like a huge opportunity to them, so I use *huge* words like *multiple continents* and *time zones* and *significant.* Then I'll look at other words the JD uses and incorporate them. "Several of my cross-functional Agile software development teams have praised my ability to design, develop, and deliver software products and transform their manual work into automated systems, including QA testing." In a single sentence, I'm able to hit upon multiple "required skills" and "key responsibilities" points in the JD.

Remember, it's my job to sell myself to them. It's not my job to convince them that this job is the best next step in my career, but rather the best possible move they could make for the sake of their own success.

Before you submit your job application, review every sentence and every word. Ask yourself, "Am I framing myself up as the ultimate candidate for this position? Or am I telling the hiring manager how excited I am about this job?" It's okay to be excited about the job and to share some of that in your application, but you don't want the hiring manager to feel like the company is doing you a favor by hiring you.

Key Takeaways

1. Don't frame a job as being perfect for *you*; frame yourself as perfect for the job.
2. Find ways to demonstrate your fit for the job. Be specific and have a couple of bullet points in all your communications.
3. Look for the intangibles like company culture and team/manager personality. Align yourself with that.
4. Be patient, humble, and confident. You will find a job.

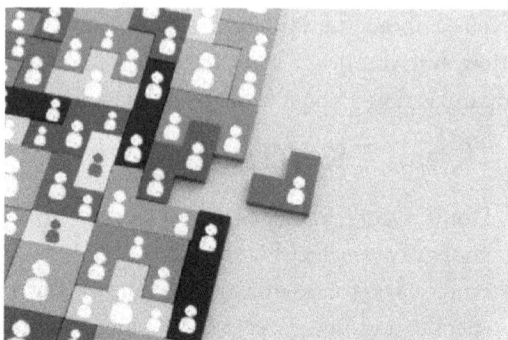

Misconception #3: Your Resume Should Represent Your Work History

AS A HIRING manager, I care about one thing: "Is this person qualified to do the job I need done?" I have read through thousands of resumes. Most of them are awful. The only time I call someone with an awful resume is when I literally have no choice because every applicant has a crappy resume. It's a lesser-of-two-evils situation.

When you're writing your resume, you're probably thinking, "They're gonna be so impressed with what I did last year. These three bullets show I'm a rock star!"

Guess what?

I rarely need a rock star. Most of the time, I need to fill my teams with people who can keep the engine running. It's great when I get someone way more capable, but for most jobs, a good hiring manager is looking for someone that can step in, get up to speed quickly, and do the job well.

You think the bullets on your resume are convincing? My guess is you're probably not even writing your resume to address the job requirements. You hand in the same resume for every application. This is another me-first way of finding a job. You're telling a bunch of hiring managers about *you* instead of describing your experience to fit the job description!

Even if your resume is beautiful, succinct, and charming, it doesn't really matter if it doesn't convince the hiring manager that you can do the job they need doing.

Tailoring your resume takes time. It is an investment and can be laborious, but if you aren't speaking the same language as the role that is posted (even if the stuff you are doing is the same stuff, but is said differently) you are missing the target. If you are really as interested in this role as you are saying with your "this role sounds as if it was written for only me" then you really should make the investment to make your resume sound that way.

What to Do

Your resume needs to reflect why *you* are the best possible candidate for this job. Make sure your resume tells the story of how you grew to the point where you are abso-freakin-lutely ready for the role.

What does that mean? Well, if you're looking for a job as a business analyst, you might not want to include any of the work experience you got as a weekend musician at your local church. If it's irrelevant to the hiring manager, then skip it. Keep it off the resume. If there are questions about a gap in your employment as a result of this omission, you can either keep the headline in without any bullets, mention in your cover letter that you're focusing on the most relevant work experience, or wait for the employer to ask about that gap.

You have nothing to lose by removing irrelevant work experience from your resume.

If a lot of your work is irrelevant and you're not left with much work history, then find ways to align those job accomplishments and requirements with the new role you're seeking. Maybe as a musician at the church, you had to manage a team of volunteers and how many hours people were committing. That's business analysis, right?

Just because the titles aren't related doesn't mean the work isn't related. (Is that a triple negative? If so, two points for Gryffindor.) Software Quality Assurance leader Tracy Olnhausen told me:

> *It really drives me crazy as a hiring manager when I get a resume that tells me what a great business analyst they are, but the cover letter tells me how they are perfect for quality assurance. You have to make sure all your materials match.*
>
> *And, I sometimes get six-page, double-sided resumes that just exhaust me.*

HR leader Vita Duncan gives this simple bit of wisdom:

> *Don't have all your accounting experience on there if you're going for a software development role.*

Simple.

Ellis has Something to Say

In my opinion, this boils down to aligning your resume content with the job description. You should have a resume version for each job type you're applying for (for example, I have one resume for content strategy and one for product marketing). Then, look at what's in the JD and make strategic changes—you don't have to redo the resume from scratch every time, otherwise you will literally spend your entire life applying for jobs.

Also, though none of the jobs I apply for require it, I still put on my resume that I speak

Mandarin. Why? It's cool, differentiating, and shows that I'm good at learning hard things.

Here's advice from external recruiter Jamie Contino:

> *It's helpful to understand the audience when submitting your resume. Most companies have internal recruiting departments and they are keyword searchers. You may be one of hundreds of applicants for one of 20+ job openings they need to fill.*
>
> *Their main question: Do you meet the basic requirements?*
>
> *It's important to know you're not the only applicant. An organized and clear outline of your skills will go miles when being reviewed by either source. At the core, the hiring team are all looking for main keywords and role descriptions to pop out at them. If your resume is too difficult to sort through, it will probably get passed over.*

Example

In much the same way as I outlined in Misconception #1's example, I'll frame my resume up in the same language and style as the JD. Let's take a look at a random JD after deleting all the unnecessary stuff, like I did in the previous chapter:

Director of Software Engineering. report into the CTO

Build, lead and grow a world-class team of software developers and quality engineers who own the execution of the product feature development programme for all products/services within the product suite using solid engineering practices.

Accountable for defining and executing on best practices, building high-performing teams, and the process necessary to have a scalable delivery model that uses both in house and external resources.

Key Responsibilities:
- leadership to the engineering teams
- robust technical engineering strategy that aligns with the needs of the business
- Establish best practice engineering and quality processes ~~to~~ reduce lead time, enhance quality/reliability
- Supervise, mentor and grow local management and engineering team
- Collaborate technically sound products on schedule with great user experience
- Drive recruiting attracting great talent and retaining

Required Skills:
- delivering SaaS solutions
- leading of Agile software development teams
- designing, developing and delivering software
- leading technical teams of 40+
- team transformation process-drive high performing team
- transforming QA to an automated model
- NET/Kubernetes/Azure/Jira

Keep in mind that this is literally the first job description I saw when I clicked the "Jobs" tab at the top of LinkedIn. It's a company based in England and I have no idea who they are. This is a truly random, hypothetical example of how I would approach the application process.

Since this role is titled Director of Software Engineering, I will likely update my previous role titles to be similar. Instead of Manager of Application Administration, I might change the title to Manager of Software Delivery, which in my industry is largely the same thing even if I didn't have that exact title. (We'll talk more about this type of manipulation in Misconception #10.)

Under that role in my current resume, I have these bullets:

- Automating global smoke tests for all production environments and building a custom Angular application for live monitoring in a NOC.
- Keeping ~40 applications online, functioning and performing under peak load for millions of users.
- Managing teams all over the world (Sri Lanka and all over the U.S.) for follow-the-sun support.
- Transitioning many applications out of captive data centers and into the cloud.
- Implementing CDN (Akamai) and APM (AppDynamics) for dozens of large-scale applications and international userbases.

The first bullet is a pretty good match for what they're asking. I might change it to say, "Automated QA tests for global execution across all production environments using in-house monitoring software I designed, developed, and delivered," because that is the exact language used in the JD.

The second bullet can be adjusted in several ways. The hiring company likely doesn't care about how many applications I administered, but they did mention scaling and SaaS, so I might incorporate some of my second bullet with my fifth. The third bullet is important, but I would modify it to better fit some of the other "key responsibilities" points.

As you can see, it takes time to adjust my resume, but once I do, I literally speak their language. I'm mirroring their terminology and selling myself as a match to their requirements.

When you're applying for a job, ask yourself, "Am I using the language the company uses and is familiar with? Will I be speaking their language or will the person reviewing my application have to translate my terminology so it matches theirs? Am I meeting them where they are or am I asking them to meet me where I am?"

Key Takeaways

1. Your resume is a sales pitch. Make sure it shows why you are the best candidate for the job.
2. Don't worry about being a rock star. Being super-competent for the job is sufficient.
3. Your resume tells the story of your career. Make it clear this position is the next chapter in your story.
4. Avoid displaying and discussing irrelevant work experience.
5. Tailor your resume for the most important jobs you want.

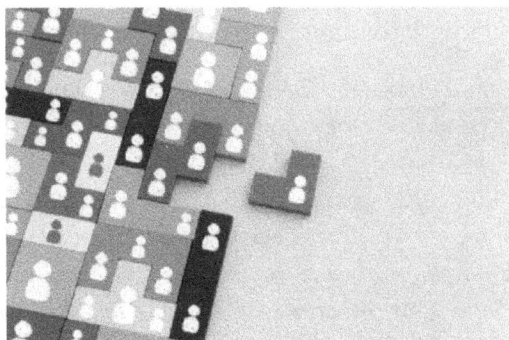

Misconception #4: The Job Description Actually Describes the Job

THIS ONE IS one of my favorites. While I have written nearly every job description for every position I've hired, most every other hiring manager I know has copy-pasted job descriptions from competing companies or from other similar job listings.

That's right: the job description you're reading is probably only 50-75% representative of the actual job you'll be doing. Maybe the hiring manager spent some time tweaking the copypasta so it's more reflective of the real work, but chances are (especially at larger companies) the description is just a generic representation of the real job.

During the interview, this is an opportunity to ask real questions about the job.

Allen Plunkett points out that you need to consider the fact that the writer of the job description likely doesn't even know what is in it.

Your excitement may not land nearly as well as you are hoping.

Ellis has Something to Say

Sometimes the job description describes what the company thinks they need, but it may not actually be what they actually need.

For example: "We need someone to manage the editorial calendar." They may not even have an editorial calendar, so they need you to figure out how to create it and fill it with content. Creating and filling an editorial calendar is way different than just managing one.

Also, use your experience to infer what's not in the description but will still likely be part of the job. For example: "Manage the editorial calendar and publish blog posts." What comes after publishing blog posts?

Promoting them!

Include those inferences in your cover letter and highlight both in your resume.

What to Do

If possible, talk to someone at the company about the job as early as possible, even before you apply. You may not be able to talk to the hiring manager directly, but there's a darn good chance you can speak with someone in HR about the job. Most times, HR (or an internal recruiter) will have more information. And if they can't answer your questions, they'll say, "I don't have those answers, but I'll talk to the hiring manager."

This always works in your favor.

First of all, you're the one making the positive first impression. Second, if you're asking smart questions, then you already look like you know what you're talking about. Third, you can tell them, "Look for my application in the next few days." Then they will know your name and you'll stand out from the rest of the applicants.

Tracy Olnhausen agrees:

> *ASK QUESTIONS ABOUT THE JOB. Maybe it isn't perfect for you, and while you might think any job is a good job right now, that isn't true. Also, if you don't ask questions and gush about the job, I will question your sanity.*

Remember, most job descriptions are copypasta. So, you might read things that conflict with one another—and you should ask about those conflicts.

If there's an opportunity to ask a follow-up question on the job description, then you look like the person who actually *read the description* and pointed out a problem. You're the expert and you make yourself look like one.

Ellis has Something to Say

> *Something else that makes you look smart is asking questions about the goals behind what's in the job description. "Why are you looking to increase leads—is it because the company isn't getting enough, or are they just not quality leads?"*
>
> *Also, make sure you have a long list of questions. Often in interviews, the interviewer will provide information that answers one or more of my questions, and it's bad to get to the end of an interview with no remaining questions to ask.*

Example

Let's go back to the JD from the previous Misconceptions and dig in. When looking at this JD, the first and foremost question I have is about the "leading of Agile software development teams." Why? Well, "Agile" has a lot of connotations and definitions vary across companies. What do they mean by "Agile?" And with their use of the capital A instead of the lowercase A, they're speaking to a specific methodology.

In software engineering, I've learned to be skeptical of companies that use "Agile" instead of "agile."

I'll have several questions to ask about this job regarding their definition of "Agile." What are they trying to accomplish? Where are they in the process of becoming "Agile?" Are they "Agile certified?" Who issued the certification? Am I expected to become certified? If I don't have a certification, does that rule me out of the job? If I have my own tweaks on the Agile process, does that disqualify me? Am I allowed to have creative freedom? The job description also mentioned alignment to best practices and standards. How far off the path are some of the teams?

Can you see how my experience in this industry leads me to a million questions about one topic and the implications of the language they're using with respect to how I'll succeed in the role?

The job description never describes the job. It describes the tip of the iceberg and reveals nothing under the water's surface. There's a reason they're hiring this role and using these specific words. It's your job to figure out why they're hiring and why they use those specific words. There's always much more to this job description than meets the eye.

When applying for a job, ask yourself, "What assumptions am I making about the job? What assumptions is the employer making that raise red flags? How do I know the job for which I'm applying is the job they're describing?"

Key Takeaways

1. Most job descriptions are copypasta. Don't believe they actually describe the job. The job may be much bigger than that.
2. Talk to someone at the company about the job before you apply. Find out as much as you can and get the company to look forward to your application.
3. Always ask questions about the job. Bring a long list of questions.
4. Don't gush about a job description the employer probably didn't even write.

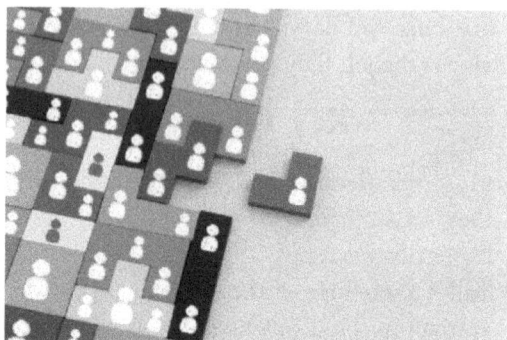

Misconception #5: Your Resume stands Out, Therefore it will get Read

MOST OF THE jobs I've posted in the past couple years have had dozens, if not hundreds, of applicants. In many cases, getting your resume reviewed is luck of the draw. Some hiring managers only look at the latest 10-15 applications in the queue. Perhaps, if you're #16, you'll get skipped over.

Some managers go in chronological order because they might feel it's more ethical to start with the people who got in line first. If you're not in the first 25 applications, then you're outta luck.

Some managers play to their biases. Perhaps they want to hire a woman, someone from their hometown, or a name that's easy to pronounce. I hate to break it to you, but even the most fair and unbiased managers play to their own biases.

Thankfully, some companies anonymize applicant metadata and withhold even the most basic information (like a name) from the hiring committee. But, this is rare.

Advice from external recruiter Allen Plunkett:

> *Don't add photos or other biographical data that could feed someone's bias. Having your resume stand out can be a good thing if you are applying*

for a creative role, but outside of having a creative resume, stick to normal formats that have the very relevant and critical information that aligns with their verbiage and information.

What to Do

Even if getting your application read is luck of the draw, it should still be engaging. Make sure it's easy to read, and that the links to your LinkedIn, website, and other relevant data are one click away. Make it easy for the hiring manager to learn as much about you as possible in 30 seconds.

Here's what I mean:

- Sentences in your cover letter are short and clear
- Bullet points on your resume aren't full of meaningless business jargon
- Your resume has enough white space and is not overloaded with text
- The links in your resume are clearly links: underlined, blue, and possibly next to relevant icons
- Your resume is no longer than two pages
- You use different typefaces appropriately; big bold text for section headers or job titles, smaller, normal text for the supporting bullets

If you have friends in the industry, ask them to look over your resume. If you get an interview with a hiring manager, you can ask whether your resume gave them all the information they needed. Get as much feedback as you can get. Search the web for resumes. See what you like. Search for people in your industry and see if you can get their resumes on their websites or by looking through their LinkedIn profiles.

There's tons of information out there. It's up to you to

find it, digest it, and reuse it for your own career advancement.

I've gotten feedback from both sides of the two-page theory of life, the universe and resumes. Some, like external recruiter Jamie Contino, say:

> *I've struggled with many senior people who limit to two pages because I need more details about what they actually did.*
>
> *The idea of a resume being condensed to two pages isn't practical. Your resume length should align to your years of experience. For example, you don't need a three-plus page resume if you've only been working for three years. But if you've been working for 10+ years, don't try to cram everything into two pages.*
>
> *A good rule of thumb [and Anthony agrees with this one]: any work experience that's farther back than eight years is okay to cut off and state: "Additional work experience available upon request." Or, simply list your titles and years of service at the different companies—no description of work needed.*

Vita Duncan tells us:

> *To avoid age bias (yes, sadly that is still a thing) resume writers ask to go back 10 years for your resume, unless the job you're applying for requires more years of experience.*

Meanwhile, other hiring managers have told me: if it's more than two pages, I probably won't get through it all. The first two pages are an indication of the rest of the resume.

My key point is: if you can't sell a hiring manager on you within the first two pages, then what difference does it make how long the resume is?

Example

I'm going to show you some screenshots of my resume, which is more an art project than it is a professional document selling myself as the ultimate candidate. You might look at this document and say, "Oh, this is cool." Or you might look at it and go, "Well, I never want to read another sentence from this guy again." That's okay. I'm good either way.

It's worth noting that my friend/boss saw this resume and said, "Anthony, no self-respecting technology expert would ever turn in a resume that looks like this." For some, this would be an insult. For me, it was a point of pride. Why?

I don't think of myself as a technology expert—I think of myself as an artist first. One advantage of recreationally interviewing is that my resume acts like a filter. Companies that appreciate a more artistic approach will appreciate my job application and are more likely to be a good fit for me. Although I am practically unemployable, I'm probably more of an acquired taste for an employer. But, if I needed a job *today*, this resume would not be a good way to approach a crowded job market.

Nevertheless, here's what my resume looks like. I'm sharing this because I want people to see that you can take multiple approaches to a job application.

My top three values are: spirituality (everyone has a unique form of expression), creativity (everyone has the capability to express themselves), and independence (I don't like anyone telling me what to do or how to express myself, so sometimes I'm rebellious). My resume is a reflection of my values. Easy for me to say, though, since I'm employed.

HELLO I'M
ANTHONY GARONE

I'm a creative technologist who solves hard problems and builds high-performance teams. Companies call on me to develop and operationalize new products or course-correct teams and projects. I'm a proven tech, culture, and innovation leader for startups, SMBs, and enterprises.

ANTHONY@GARONE.ORG
TWITTER: @ATGARONE
LINKEDIN: /ANTHONYGARONE
CELL: +1 480-

FULL-TIME WORK

DIRECTOR OF EMERGING PRODUCT DELIVERY, INFOARMOR
2018 - PRESENT

- Brought new Allstate Digital Footprint and Privacy features to market
- Key leader for digital transformation efforts (with ThoughtWorks)
- Provided solutions for complex enterprise client partnerships and integrations
- Delivered next-gen external APIs, user portal, and mobile apps
- Led through acquisition, rapidly scaled department from 15 to ~90 FTEs
- Built Solutions Architecture, Developer Advocacy, and Innovation teams
- Stabilized product development/delivery with CI/CD, staffing

TECH DIRECTOR, MELTMEDIA
2013 - 2018

- Executive tech leader over IT, QA, front- and back-end dev
- Introduced automation workflows for test, build, and deploy
- Generated & grew business (referred/closed over $750K in new business)
- Intentionally reduced team size/budget by ~$1M and increased productivity
- Organized people/teams around skills, mentorship, and goals
- Automated and visualized business operations data and results
- Overhauled talent pipeline and recruitment processes
- Under-promise and over-deliver on ~100 concurrent client projects

TECHNICAL MANAGER, PEARSON
2007 - 2013

- Managed infrastructure, deployments, and BCP/DR for ~40 global products
- Proposed, created, and led integration engineering and automation teams
- Automated multi-vendor public, private, and hybrid cloud provisioning
- Led and ran major Application Performance Monitoring implementation
- Managed programs and projects for data center and cloud migrations
- Worked closely with Chinese government and Pearson execs on Akamai Web Application Acceleration deployment for English language learning
- Increased team efficiency up to 10x without new headcount via automation

TWITTER: @ATGARONE · LINKEDIN: /ANTHONYGARONE

PART-TIME WORK

AUTHOR, <u>STAIRWAY PRESS</u>
2019 - PRESENT

- *Clueless at The Work: Advice from a Corporate Tyrant*, Sept. 2019
  - Provides a framework for professional development and success
- *Failure to Fracture: Learning King Crimson's Impossible Song*, Summer 2020
  - A 22-year study of transformation to play "impossible" music

FOUNDER, <u>MAKE WEIRD MUSIC</u>
2014 - PRESENT

- Host and promote concerts with the world's most creative artists
- Video and audio production, engineering, editing, mixing, and mastering
- Interview artists virtually and in-person for video and podcasts
- Custom illustrations and transcriptions for every release
- Sell merchandise and creative services to an international audience

ADVISOR, <u>MUSIC TRAVELER</u>
2019-PRESENT

- Provide CTO services and direction to executive team and advisory board
- Strategically direct mobile and web application development
- Assist with sponsors and partner relationship development

CO-FOUNDER, ENTREPRENEUR
2015 - 2018

- <u>Kensho Education</u>
  - Write and teach self-awareness courses for professionals
  - Host classes in-house or at corporate offices
- <u>Jargone</u>
  - Reframe corporate job descriptions as marketing tools
  - Rewrite awful job descriptions for fun and money

EDUCATION

MS TECHNOLOGY MANAGEMENT
2010 Arizona State University

BS COMPUTER SCIENCE
2004 Arizona State University

ADVISORY WORK

STARTUPS AND ARIZONA COLLEGES

- 2015 - Present, **Chairman**: Arizona State University's Graphic Information Technology
- 2018-19: GoCoach, stand-in CTO, developer, technology advisor
- 2015-18, Member: Mesa Community College, Maricopa Corporate College, South Mountain Community College, University of Advancing Technology

VALUES

SPIRITUALITY
I need to have "soul in the game" when it comes to work. My work helps give me purpose and I see it as an extension of myself.

CREATIVITY
No matter what I am doing, I need to find some element of creativity to feel great about it.

INDEPENDENCE
It's very important that I have the freedom to use my creativity to solve a problem. I work best when I'm trusted to succeed without micromanagement.

BELIEFS & ETHICS

BOOKS AND DOCUMENTS THAT HAVE SHAPED MY APPROACH

Mindset (Dweck)
Antifragile and Fooled by Randomness (Taleb)
Fifth Discipline (Senge)
Thinking, Fast and Slow (Kahneman)
Good Business and Creativity (Czikszentmihalyi)
Predictably Irrational (Ariely)
Netflix culture
Pre-suasion and Influence (Cialdini)
Power and Leadership BS (Pfeffer)
Crucial Conversations (Grenny)
Five Dysfunctions of a Team (Lencioni)
Managing Oneself (Drucker)
Acceptance, commitment (Forsyth)
The Prisoner (McGoohan)
Science of Mindfulness (Siegel)
The Alliance (Hoffman)

TWITTER: @ATGARONE · LINKEDIN: /ANTHONYGARONE

Key Takeaways

1. There's no way of knowing how and when resumes will be reviewed. Don't bet on being an early applicant or the latest applicant.
2. There will be bias in how resumes are selected. Don't make your resume stand out with photos or flash unless it's necessary.
3. Make it easy for a hiring manager to know you in 30 seconds.
4. Get feedback on your resume however you can get it.
5. Don't worry about length. Or do worry about it. Who knows?

Misconception #6: Hiring Managers Know How to Hire

A MAJORITY OF the managers I know became managers because they were good at something. That *something* was probably not management.

A lot of the time, in order to "move up the ladder," they take management roles. But there's a huge difference between being great at sweeping floors and being great at running a team that sweeps floors.

As such, you can't assume hiring managers are objective, fair, or even very good at hiring. You can only hope the hiring managers know talent when they see it. (Hint: They probably don't.)

Worse, sometimes hiring managers inherit teams without any semblance of understanding of the work the teams are doing.

How do I know this?

Because I am this!

I ran a team where I barely understood what was happening day-to-day and I had to trust my team's judgment that they're doing things right. Feedback from other teams was essential to inform me of my team's success.

And if you think I'm being dramatic about this

misconception, I'll point you to Jamie Contino's thoughts on this section: "Preach!"

What to Do

See if you can find the name of the hiring manager for the position you're targeting. Look them up on LinkedIn or social media. All of this information is public and can be used to your advantage. You might even try messaging them to get a conversation started. Tell them you're interested in the position and want to do everything possible to address all the major requirements of the role.

It's nearly impossible to determine whether someone is a good hiring manager, but if they write recommendations for their peers and teammates on LinkedIn (or have some written about them), that's a good sign.

From CTO and sales executive Marquess Lewis:

> *Unless the company has invested in real recruiting coaching, hiring managers don't know how to hire. Know and be prepared for both those who don't and a few who do.*
>
> *Talk about real situations—the situation and the business context, what YOU did, and include the outcome. Not that the code got written, or the bug got fixed, but that a customer was retained, customer satisfaction was increased or costs were cut. Real outcomes.*

Example

You might ask yourself, "How does this guy know hiring managers don't know how to hire?"

Because they tell me!

Probably 10 times in 2020 alone, I stepped in to hire for

positions that did not report to me. I've even had friends who run other companies ask me to step in and hire on their behalf.

Hiring is hard and hiring managers know it.

To make it easier for the hiring manager and for yourself, here are tactics I recommend:

1. Ask, "What are some specific criteria you're using to hire for this position?"
2. Ask, "Do you have any specific questions about my work experience that could address concerns or gaps you have about hiring me?"
3. Provide written documentation and evidence that substantiate your claims. The moment you've got an interview scheduled, tell the scheduler that you have a portfolio or some documentation relevant to your application that you'd like to discuss at the interview.
   a. Written recommendations and emails with great professional feedback are fantastic.
   b. Documentation samples (that are stripped of proprietary information!) demonstrate the quality of work you do before they work with you.
   c. References to work-related volunteer projects, open-source projects, or non-profit organizations can be helpful.
4. Ask who will be conducting your interview and research them before you meet. Find a way to break the ice in your interview based on that research.
   a. Do not stalk! Stick to LinkedIn and professional sources.

The point is to make it as easy as possible for the hiring manager to say, "This person knows what they're doing. It's a no-brainer."

Key Takeaways

1. The hiring manager may not know what they're doing. Be as clear and proactive as you can.
2. Focus on business outcomes to show your impact. Anyone can finish their work; not everyone can link it to real results.
3. Try to determine the hiring manager's personal pain points. They say they really need someone who can self-manage? Provide examples.

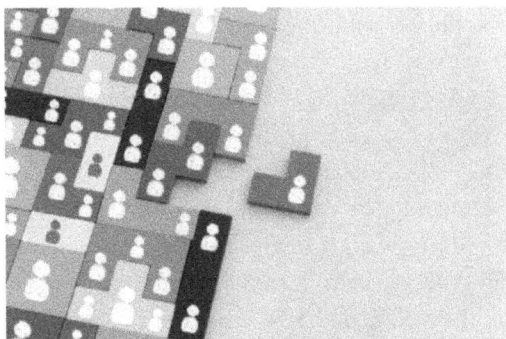

Misconception #7: Internal Recruiters Know Who They're Looking For

INTERNAL RECRUITERS ARE wonderful. They save hiring managers so much time.

Instead of having to look through every resume and spend hours every day looking for that perfect candidate, a hiring manager can ask an internal recruiter, "Can you send me resumes that meet these qualifications?"

I've worked with several internal recruiters and they've been lifesavers.

They ask me questions like, "Tell me about the kinds of people you're looking to hire." Or, "How can I tell a good candidate from a lesser one?" Or, "What are some of the keywords you expect to come up in conversation with a good candidate?" Or, "What are some questions you'd like me to ask the candidate and what are answers you would expect to hear from a good candidate?"

Internal recruiters have saved me countless hours, especially after my employer was acquired for half a billion dollars and I had to help my department scale from 15 people to 90 in just a few months while also working my regular full-time gig.

The internal recruiters made sure I only spoke to

39

qualified candidates who met the specific criteria I requested, and I met weekly with them to get updated on the kinds of people who were applying. Even better, the recruiters would send me a few LinkedIn profiles and say, "Does this person represent a good candidate for the role?"

Unfortunately for you, internal recruiters are rarely experts for the positions being hired. They generally have a Human Resources background and rarely have expertise outside of their domain (HR is complicated and a universe unto itself!), so if you're a technology person, the recruiter is probably flying blind trying to figure out how to be helpful. They don't necessarily have an eye for the perfect candidate and need a lot of help. They're lifesavers for hiring managers, but probably a little difficult for the candidates due to their lack of expertise.

For example, Vita Duncan told us:

> *As a recruiter, when I was reviewing resumes, I would always make sure the candidate met the minimum qualifications of the job. In your resume, clearly state your highest level of education and years of experience.*

Vita knows she's not always the right person to evaluate someone's specific skills within a non-HR discipline.

Make technical evaluations easy for her and other recruiters.

What to Do

If you're working with an internal recruiter, find ways to help them understand the job better and why you're going to make their lives easier.

For example, if you're applying for a project management role, you might ask questions like:

- What can you tell me about the current project portfolio?
- What project management methodologies does the company use?
- Is this role part of a formal PMO (Project Management Office) or is it matrixed into another department?
- How many concurrent projects might I expect to manage once I am up and running?
- How important are project management certifications at the company?

These questions might overwhelm the recruiter, so you can reframe some of them.

For example:

- "I prefer to use a Kanban project management approach. I've also done waterfall and Agile. Do you know what methodologies I'd be using in this role?"
- "In my current role, I report to a Director of Project Management who oversees about 30 projects at one time. Would I report to someone in a similar role with a similar portfolio?"
- "I'm used to working with two to three teams at one time on four to five concurrent projects with weekly project status meetings. Does that sound like the kind of pace I'd experience in this role?"

Not only do you get to share what you're doing, but you get to pre-load the recruiter with some good questions to ask the hiring manager.

Chances are, your name will be associated with these above and beyond questions and may improve your odds at getting eyes on your application.

You might even say to the recruiter: "Would you be able to answer some technical questions I have about the role?" Some recruiters will say, "I'd be happy to relay your questions to the hiring manager," or you might even get lucky if they say, "I'd be happy to get you in touch with the hiring manager for that."

A word of warning from Tracy Olnhausen:

> *Be careful not to talk your way out of the job by talking to HR. They rarely have a clue what I am looking for in a candidate. I usually ask them NOT to screen resumes because they don't understand technical jobs.*

And advice from Jamie Contino:

> *Make the hiring manager's job easier. Be engaged, thoughtful, and don't waste their time. They are the gatekeepers to your new career.*

From recruiter Allen Plunkett:

> *Internal recruiters can help with understanding the company's leadership style, culture, environment, and what makes them get up every day and report for duty there.*
>
> *When you engage with the internal recruiter, you are doing something more unique than you think. Often potential candidates see recruiters as a cog in the wheel—"I just need to*

get past this person so that I can get to the real interview" is an approach that a lot of people (who ultimately don't get hired) take. Don't be one of those people.

Recruiters filter someone who is rude, flippant, or too casual. Take advantage of the fact that they know the hiring managers, the backgrounds of people who have been hired and retained, and likely some of the pain points inside the team and the org. They can be a wealth of information if you engage and treat them as a source of insight and perspective.

Recruiters love being an information source, but you won't get what you don't ask for. They are gauging your level of interest and if you ask no questions of them, then you must not be interested.

Key Takeaways

1. Internal recruiters likely don't understand the ins and outs of your job. If you talk to one, ask questions that show you understand what the job means without completely overwhelming them.
2. Don't go too far the other way! If you try to go into detail explaining the job *they* are hiring for, you'll come off as arrogant (or, depending on gender dynamics, a mansplainer. Don't be a mansplainer).
3. Demonstrate your interest and engage with the internal recruiter. They have a lot of good information and have a lot of power. Treat them accordingly.

Misconception #8: Your Work Speaks for Itself

YOU MIGHT THINK you're the cock of the walk because you completed the big dingus project at your last company. It's right at the top of your resume—the first bullet under the most current job. "Took ownership and saw Project Dingus to completion, on time and on budget."

Oh yeah, that's the stuff.

The hiring manager has no idea what you're talking about.

What is Project Dingus?

Why should anyone care?

If you can't articulate the business impact of the work you do, you might as well write your resume in Swahili; it'd make just as much sense to the hiring manager.

You need to talk about your work in generic, easy-to-understand terms. You can, of course, use relevant keywords that a resume skimmer will pick up (could be a computer, could be a recruiter, could be the hiring manager).

There's tons of evidence saying that if you're a woman, you're far less likely to speak up about your work. If you think that's you, I highly encourage listening to a podcast called

Advice to My Younger Me, episode 13 with Tara Mohr.[3]

She says that women, especially when competing with men, need to speak up to make their work visible to others.

Advice from recruiter Allen Plunkett:

> *Use metrics, like showing how much revenue you created as a result of being the head dingus or...the processes you improved and how that translated into money. Another reason you need to mimic the words in the job description is because your company may well say dingus when every other company in your industry says the exact same thing, but their word is flatus—hate to see someone not get hired just because their dingus is actually a flatus. Seen it happen a million times.*

Tracy Olnhausen points out:

> *If you put a ton of metrics in your resume, be ready to back them up. You saved the company $1 million? You better be able to back that up!*

Vita Duncan notes:

> *Managers also like quantifiable information in your resume. Like, 'I saved _____ on Project X.' Be prepared to explain how you did it.*

Such good advice. Quantify your success. It's nice that you did something, but it's better when you can demonstrate the

---

[3] https://tomyyounger.me/episode-13-get-rid-of-old-habits-to-play-a-bigger-game/

impact of what you did!

Carmen West reminds us of what these quantifications can do for us:

> Your resume should remind you of your value and renew faith in yourself. You've done all of this before. It's nothing new.
>
> Reviewing it might help you remember some things you forgot about. With that passion and faith, you have to understand you can get through anything. If you can get through the challenges of the past 5 or 10 years, what makes you think you can't get through your next role? You can!
>
> You just need to be reminded of that with the raw data. Sitting down with your resume and going through the journey reminds you of that and gives you the tenacity and boldness you need for that interview. That's important.

Ellis has Something to Say

> As a woman, speaking up for your work can be difficult, especially since on the job, you can enlist an advocate.
>
> But, on the job interview, you're the only one who can speak up for you. One issue I've encountered a few times is that my work will be hidden behind someone else's name (often, but not always, a man's).
>
> When speaking about such a project, bring up the project's success, what exactly you did and how, and where necessary note that the byline/credit went to an executive, i.e. the byline wasn't an exhaustive list of collaborators.

46

What to Do

There are a couple aspects to getting your work in front of the eyes of hiring managers: gaming the system, and addressing reality. There are several ways of gaming the system. Let's start there.

Recruiters search for candidates primarily via LinkedIn. They often start with relevant keywords. For an accounting position, they might search for terms like EBITDA, CPA, SOX (Sarbanes-Oxley), compliance, or GAAP.

Recruiters often pay for a special version of LinkedIn that's optimized for finding job candidates. They can tell if you have the checkbox filled in that says you're open for work. They might prioritize those people and look at where they're located, years of experience, degrees of separation/mutual connections, etc.

I have a keywords section buried in my LinkedIn profile. It's at the bottom of my About section. I literally have a paragraph that says, Keywords: consultant, solutions architect, sales engineer, software, etc. There is a character limit on the field, so max that sucker out. Then, when a recruiter searches for solutions architect, even if it's nowhere in your work experience, you'll show up in the search results.

Another way of gaming the system involves secretly packing your resume and cover letter with keywords relevant to the job itself.

Companies often use an Applicant Tracking System (ATS) to manage job postings and applicants. Those ATSs often come with resume parsing capabilities that will score a job application by its content.

So, if you upload a PDF resume, you can pile all those keywords into some PDF metadata fields (Preview.app on the Mac offers a metadata field right in the Save As... dialog).

Some ATSs are smart enough to ignore that, so some

applicants will put all the keywords in the PDF itself in invisible text. They'll actually put a lot of keywords in the document as size 0, white text so the keywords are visible to the ATS scanner and not to a human. Again, there are ATSs that are smart enough to ignore (or even penalize) applicants who do this, so be careful with your use of this tactic.

Enough about gaming the system; let's address reality.

You might have to reframe the work you've done so it aligns with what the hiring manager is requesting in the job description.

For example, I applied for a job that said something like...

> We are looking for a leader to help us scale our company from 30 people to 100 in a short amount of time. This person needs to invest in each existing hire as well as shepherd each new hire into the growing company without discomfort.

So what did I do?

I made sure my resume and cover letter started out with examples of how I scaled companies to meet business needs in short amounts of time. I talked about my first book, *Clueless at The Work*, and how it was inspired by tons of employees asking me to write down all the topics we'd discussed in our 1:1 meetings and coaching sessions. I framed up my application so it met the hiring manager where he needed me to be.

I was asked for an interview a few days later. Nearly all of the questions he asked me were about scaling and the experience I'd mentioned in my cover letter and resume. I brought attention to my relevant accomplishments first and foremost in writing, and made sure it was the primary topic of discussion. I let the work I'd done steer the conversation.

Key Takeaways

1. Know how to strategically position the work that you've done so that it speaks directly to what the company is looking for.
2. Articulate the business impact of your work. Don't know what it is? Think about how it fit into the department and company strategy, and tie it into that.
3. Game the system in an honest way: optimize your LinkedIn profile About section with keywords to the max.
4. Think about if you want to game the system by adding keywords to metadata or invisibly to your resume. Be sure you're ready to accept the potential penalties.
5. Articulate the business impact of your work. That's not a mistake, that's repetition for effect.

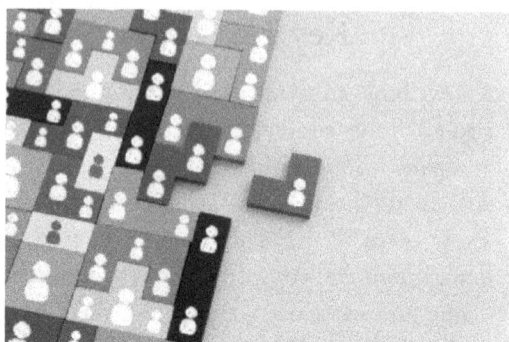

Misconception #9: You Know How to Explain What You've Done

PICTURE THIS: YOU'RE in a job interview with a hiring manager and they say, "I saw on your resume that you were the project lead for Project Dingus. Can you tell me more about that?"

What are you going to say? Are you going to make something up real quick? Or maybe you have a great story about Project Dingus up your sleeve.

You look the hiring manager right in the eyes and say, "Uh...yeah, I was the lead on Project Dingus. We got it done on time. It was pretty cool."

Ouch.

Or maybe you told this big, long story that was so contextual there's no way the hiring manager could understand what you're talking about. They just start nodding and try to follow along until you're finished. Also ouch.

Listen, I'm sure you're smart and telling the truth about everything on your resume. You probably really did (or do) an awesome job or something on that Project Dingus.

In my experience, however, most people aren't good at telling stories. And they're really not good at seeing the larger story arcs in their own lives. You may be the exception, but don't count on it. Candidates have to spend a lot of time thinking about how everything fits together and how to package that up into a story to share at an interview.

For example, if an interviewer asked you to share the hardest problem you've had to solve in the last few years, would you be able to tell a compelling story?

Would you be able to explain the importance of the task? Or even make your accomplishment sound important?

A great candidate needs to sound like a great hire. Talking about all your previous work as though it's no big deal or without any sort of connection to the overall team/department/company mission can make you sound disconnected from your work's purpose.

Most hiring managers aren't going to easily or quickly understand the impact of your prior work without you setting up a story. They'll need context, characters, drama, conflict, and resolution.

I can't tell you how many interviews I've conducted where I'll ask for an explanation of something on the candidate's resume.

Most of the time, I received an improvised response that misses an opportunity to tell me a story of accomplishment.

But, man, that Project Dingus was crazy amazing.

What to Do

Use your cover letter and resume to tell a meaningful story that gets the attention of whoever is reviewing your job application.

It doesn't have to be long or particularly detailed.

For example, if the job you want is a project lead, your resume can say: "Worked closely with the project lead on Project Flargen ($3.4M budget, major company initiative)."

Your cover letter can say, "I am ready to become a project lead. On Project Flargen, I worked hand in hand with

Anthony Garone and Ellis Fitch

the project lead. It was my responsibility to ensure the project was completed on time, which required coordination with 34 teams across 87 time zones. I would love to tell you more about this at an interview."

Then at the interview, you can either wait for the hiring manager to mention Project Flargen or you can say, "I wanted to talk to you about my role on Project Flargen. I think it's a great representation of what I can bring to the team as a project lead." Hopefully the interviewer will acquiesce and be wowed by your incredible conversational prowess.

It can't hurt to memorize one or two versions of the same story. Write the stories down and edit them to death. Make every word count.

One version can be 30 seconds long and another can be 60. Practice telling these stories to friends. (Don't be embarrassed. A good friend will want to help you get a job.) Make sure your friends understand the story.

Practice telling it to people outside your industry and ask if it made any sense. Record yourself with your cell phone and time yourself. Make sure you know how to tell the story without mistakes.

Practice when you're alone and practice when you're in a highly interruptive environment.

Do everything you can to prepare yourself for an opportunity to explain what you've done, why it's significant, and why you are the best candidate for the job.

As Jamie reminds us:

If it's on your resume, it's fair game to ask about. Have a basic 30-60 second pitch and then ask if more detail is needed. Be prepared to provide this detail in a concise manner.

52

Ellis has Something to Say

Frame your explanations like a story, but corporate style. Here's how I like to think of the framing:

Problem > Goal > Your plan > Your role in the plan > How you executed > What were the results? > Learnings

Example

The other day, my 13-year-old son came into my office and said, "Dad, what is your actual job?"

To be honest, I could barely give him an answer. My wife likes to joke, "I have no idea what you do and I can barely explain it. I just tell people that you work in software."

Realistically, this is a good litmus test.

If I can't explain to my family members what I do, will I be able to explain it succinctly to my next hiring committee?

Probably not.

When writing a cover letter or speaking to points on your resume, you need to be able to explain it to a 6th grader.

What if you're being interviewed by someone from another department who doesn't fully understand what you do? What if you need to explain to an internal recruiter who knows to listen for the right keywords, but doesn't understand the work itself?

In that case, you have a great opportunity to flex your communication muscle and get an *in* with whoever's selecting you.

For each of the key bullets in your resume, write a couple of sentences in a preparation document that meaningfully explains what you're trying to say. Then practice explaining it to your non-expert family members or friends.

Ultimately, I told my son, "You know all those online

applications you use for virtual school? I help make applications like those, keep them updated with cool features, and make sure they stay online. I also help sell our products to other companies who want to buy them."

My son looked at me and said, "Um, okay."

Then he asked if he could play Fortnite.

C'est la vie.

Key Takeaways

1. Prepare anecdotes about key projects. Frame them like a story and make yourself the hero.
2. Corporate storytelling goes like this: Problem > Goal > Your plan > Your role in the plan > How you executed > What were the results? > Learnings.
3. Practice telling these stories.
4. Keep them short. Two minutes is too long. Especially on phone interviews, people will tune you out quickly.

Misconception #10: All the Other Candidates are Telling the Truth

YOU KNOW HOW many people have lied on their job applications about their past successes? Um, countless. I've probably done it myself, perhaps even intentionally. The thing is, there are millions of people looking for jobs and they want the job perhaps as much as you do. You think they're going to let honesty get in the way? Pah!

Sometimes I can tell someone is lying on their resume just by their career path. "Oh, this person graduated from college five years ago, was a network administrator for three years, and then became Senior Director of Network Administration at a major corporation? Sounds legit." Those applications go straight into the trash. Well, sometimes I share them with my peers so we can all laugh first.

Worse, sometimes I know what they're lying about. They'll take credit for work they obviously couldn't do or work I know someone else did. Believe me, I do a lot of networking and I hear a lot of stories. I've even called people out in interviews and said, "I see you did X on this project. I happen to know the project lead over there and she couldn't recall you contributing in this way." It's a nice way to see how the candidate will handle being called out on BS.

What to Do

You can't control what other people put on their resumes. So, what can you do to compete? I'll let Ellis take that one.

Ellis has Something to Say

Be the best, truest version of yourself (until misconception #11).

Don't lie to one-up all the people out there who might lie. Use the tips in this book to position yourself to your greatest advantage. If a company hires a liar, they're going to realize it was a bad choice when they a. uncover the lie or b. realize this person doesn't have the experience they were looking for in the first place.

Focus on yourself, your experience, and your application and interview.

Back to Anthony: I agree with Ellis. Whether others lie is of no concern.

Whether you are a badass is.

Key Takeaways

1. Don't lie.
2. Be awesome.
3. Prove it.

Misconception #11: You Must be Completely Honest

LET'S GET THINGS straight: I am not saying you should be dishonest on your resume. However, you need to be willing to play with the truth. For example, let's say you have a degree in Computer Science, but the job description says a degree in Computer Systems Engineering is required. Is it dishonest to say you have a degree in Computer Systems Engineering? Well, kinda, but not really.

Here's the thing: different schools have different names for similar programs. At one school, a CSE degree may be hardware-focused. At another, a CSE degree may focus more on tactical, practical applications. Some engineering schools offer Computer Science degrees that are 95% theory and 5% programming, where other schools have it the other way around. If you're in a field like Marketing, it's an even bigger tossup.

Sure, they want someone with a degree in journalism, English, or related field, but really, they just want to know that you went to college (and even if you didn't, it isn't always a nail in the coffin). What they really want to know is, "Are you competent at your job?"

Heck, I don't even know what's written on my master's

degree because the freaking university changed the name of the program three times while I was enrolled!

Do you want to let the name of your degree stop you from getting that job? Unless you're 100% confident they're going to call your college to see the exact words on the diploma, I say it's perfectly fine to make your degree be the same as what's listed in the job requirements.

The title of your college degree is just one aspect of your history. There will be other areas with flexibility, like job titles (systems administrator vs. application administrator, social media manager vs. social media analyst, etc.), where you can take some creative liberties.

The point is not to lie, but to fit the expectations of the employer. Consider terminology they already know and reduce the need to explain yourself.

Ellis has Something to Say

I hesitantly support this message. My college diploma is written in Latin and I have been asked to provide both the degree and the certified translation. My mother, a professional decades out of college, has also been asked to provide her degree. Like, recently. Tread carefully.

Everything on my resume is totally true. Maybe this is why Anthony is way more successful than I am.

What to Do

Is everyone guilty of stretching the truth on their resume? I know I've done it and my anecdotal evidence tells me that everyone else does it, too. It's a fact of life. The truth is: most of the work we do is boring. Answering emails, attending lame meetings, listening to some corporate suit drone on from his summer home about how tough things have been.

The thing is, there's a difference between *lying* and *framing the truth*. Actually lying is saying you have a degree you do not have or making it look like you completed a degree when you really didn't. I know a guy who put the following on his resume: "1983-1987 Glendale Community College, B.A. Accounting." He never finished the degree, but he did study for four years in the accounting program. I told him he was *lying*, but he just laughed it off.

Manipulating the truth gets to the fact that there's no material difference between what you're saying and what the hiring manager wants to hear. To use the previous example, if the difference between a Computer Science degree and a Computer Systems Engineering degree is only two or three classes, does it truly matter if you put one or the other on the resume? Chances are your job has already given you the real world experience covered in those few classes you didn't take.

Actually lying:

- Saying you are a volunteer member of a board when you're not
- Saying you speak a language when you cannot
- Saying you attended a university when you did not
- Saying you got a diploma when you did not
- Saying you worked somewhere you did not

Manipulating the truth:

- Rounding up your salary to the nearest $5K or $10K (Look up "anchor points" in negotiation books)
- Exaggerating the extent to which you know a person in your network
- Slightly changing your previous job titles so they tell a better career trajectory story

- Exaggerating your expertise with a tool or technology you haven't used in a couple years

You need to ask yourself, though: is it worth getting caught? Why are you thinking of lying or stretching the truth? What's the longer-term effect of editing the facts? Can you do this in good conscience?

Jamie Contino, an external recruiter, says:

> *I would err on the side of truthfulness. Most companies have core values that revolve around integrity, so I'd stick to the truth or just don't put it in your resume. Better: Make your resume so compelling they want to talk to you regardless of the degree you had.*
>
> *And it is okay to embellish the details/responsibilities of your role if you actually performed these at some point (maybe you were an out of office for someone and acted on their behalf? Or perhaps you wore multiple hats until a new person was hired?).*

Key Takeaways

1. Don't lie.
2. If you must exaggerate the truth, do it cautiously and wisely. If you're going to embellish, don't go beyond verifiable facts.
3. Lies of omission do not count as "exaggerating the truth."
4. If you're wondering whether you should exaggerate or not, play out the scenario where the hiring manager finds out. Is it a minor embarrassment you can work through, or are you toast? Don't be toast.

Misconception #12: Job Requirements are Requirements

FUNNY THING ABOUT the word *requirements*. You'd think they're absolutely necessary. Well, let me blow your freaking mind...

Job requirements are not actual requirements.

I have hired great candidates who barely met the requirements. If you're thinking about applying for a job where the requirements seem out of reach, then you're probably not qualified for the job. But if you understand the requirements and have a good sense of why the requirements are in the job description, then you're probably qualified.

Why do these requirements get put in the job description? Remember what I said about most descriptions being copypasta? Well, there's only a few templates for a job description and most of them look like this:

- Company overview
- Job overview
- Responsibilities
- Requirements
- Nice-to-haves

Sometimes the requirements are just something someone else came up with and the hiring manager thought, "Well, that sounds good enough." As Jamie Contino says, hiring managers are typically after 80% alignment with the requirements.

What to Do

Like I said, many jobs have requirements that aren't actual requirements. They're remnants of copypasta. I like to compare JD requirements to the old "letter of the law versus the spirit of the law" argument. In most cases I've encountered, *especially* at smaller companies, the letter of the JD doesn't matter as much as the spirit of the JD. Like I said earlier, if you think you're qualified for a role and you understand the spirit of the JD, then apply. Use your judgment.

Your cover letter and resume should give the hiring manager all the proof they need. But if those are weak, then you won't be convincing enough to make it past the basic gatekeeping criteria.

In short: if you're close, apply.

From CTO and sales executive Marquess Lewis:

> Very often the requirements are a set of impossible expectations—sometimes the hiring manager or firm understands that and knows that they are going to have to make a tradeoff, other times not. Sometimes, they are intentionally a fishing expedition to find out if the unicorn they'd like to have actually exists.
>
> Just because you can't punch every box doesn't mean you shouldn't apply; a strong candidate will explain to me how those other requirements can get met or where they might sit

better in the org (after asking some thoughtful questions about the role).

Ellis has Something to Say

When Anthony and I worked in the same office, I sometimes overheard his side of the phone conversation when he was interviewing candidates. The one I remember most was the interview that was painfully short. I heard Anthony ask a very specific question, something like, "How would you design a reusable component in this language?"

Then he asked the same question two or three more times in a slightly different way. The call ended less than five minutes later. This person clearly did not meet all the requirements, but got through anyway.

If that guy can get an interview, SO CAN YOU.

Example

Let's take a look at another totally random job description I found on LinkedIn. This job is with a technology provider in the healthcare industry.

Requirements:

- Minimum 2 years of experience in complex project management in a healthcare and IT setting.
- Bachelor's Degree (Healthcare, Health Informatics preferred) or a combination of college education and 5-7 years of relevant experience.
- Proficiency in Microsoft Project or similar system preferred.

- Candidates with Epic certification, prior Epic Install Experience preferred.
- Experience with Interoperability and/or Interface/HL7 will be given preference.
- PMP certification preferred.
- Proven success in internal and external communication and relationship management with all levels of expertise from administrative to executive.
- Technical aptitude to fully understand and gain the necessary knowledge required to effectively collaborate with members.
- 2,000-5,000 hours leading and managing projects desired.

Okay, let's take a look...

Why are they asking for 2 years of experience in complex project management in addition to 5-7 years of "relevant experience?" Well, since they work with healthcare providers, they probably handle a lot of personally identifiable information, which is not only highly sensitive but highly regulated. HIPAA violations are hecka expensive! So, they want someone with at least 5 years of experience, including 2 years of complex project management work.

I probably wouldn't apply for this job unless I had at least 5 years experience, just based on those lines alone. But if I had 4 years, I might make a strong case in my cover letter about the experience I've gained in my short time in the role. Or, if I've transitioned from another career/industry, I would use those years of experience to justify my applying.

A Bachelor's degree? They probably want to get a candidate that really knows and understands healthcare. If I didn't have a degree, I'd lean on any healthcare-related experience in my past. And if I didn't have that, I'd skip applying.

Proficiency in Microsoft Project or similar system. So, they're using software to manage their project schedule, budget, and resource allocation. I'd apply if I had any experience using an enterprise-worthy project management application (even online ones like Smartsheet) and I could show robust, in-depth knowledge of the tool. If I didn't have Microsoft Project experience (or a certification), I'd really need to lean on my experience in tracking budget, timeline, scope, dependencies and other project-specific work to compensate.

Epic certification? I don't even know what that is, so I'll skip that.

Interoperability and/or interface/HL7? A quick search for "HL7" reveals it is the name of the organization that publishes the FHIR, a healthcare-related data exchange standard. I personally don't have experience in such things, but if I had experience with similar data exchange frameworks, I would mention that and try to find a way to align that with what HL7 has published. Chances are that other data exchange specifications would be analogous, so I would lean on that experience. But since they're getting this specific, I'm thinking I probably wouldn't be the best candidate for this role.

I'm not ruling myself out yet, though!

PMP certification? Well, it turns out I used to have one of those. It stands for Project Management Professional and is highly valued by some organizations. It requires continuous learning credits to keep the credential active, which I did not do. However, the fact that I used to be PMP-certified is worth noting in my cover letter.

Proven success in internal and external communication and relationship management?

Sure.

I can talk about how I've worked with executives,

individual contributors, and all levels of middle management to get my job done.

Technical aptitude?

I have no concerns.

I've never been involved with a project and been unable to grasp what's going on, even in highly technical and complex situations.

2,000-5,000 hours? Meh. Good luck proving any of that. The only time people track their hours like that are for credentials (like the PMP).

And it's all loose math.

I can say, "Well, I do project work 35 hours every week, so I'll multiply that by 8 months, carry the 1, drop the remainder, and voila! I've got 1,200 hours or so of experience."

Yes, that is literally how I was told to calculate my PMP hours before I was certified.

So, yeah, the requirements on this job are easily negotiable. Now, maybe they have a super strict hiring manager over this role, or there's some compliance organization that strictly tracks numbers and candidate qualifications. In that case, my application will probably get tossed.

Otherwise, I think I have a solid argument in my favor for the employer to put me in their role.

Key Takeaways

1. Requirements are more like suggestions. If you're close, apply.
2. Show why you're a strong candidate. Dazzle in your resume and cover letter.

Misconception #13: You Shouldn't Ask Your Friends to Help Get You an Interview at Their Company

THERE'S AN OLD saying: "It's not *what* you know, but *who* you know." And let me tell you, that is 100% true. If you have a friend who works at a company that has a job opening and you're not asking that friend for some inside information, you are being stupid.

Yes, I went there. Stupid.

The world runs on relationships.

If your friend is in good standing at the company, the hiring manager is going to feel *way* better about interviewing you because your friend trusts you. This is one of those "the friend of my friend is a friend to me" situations. Don't shortchange yourself because you feel like it's awkward or inappropriate.

Ask kindly and don't have expectations.

All you have to say is, "Hey friend, I'm thinking of applying for a job at your company. Any chance you know anything about the role or the team or the hiring manager?"

Easy.

And if the company gives a referral bonus, it's extra

incentive to leverage every connection you have.

From CTO and sales executive Marquess Lewis:

> *The number one issue in my opinion is that someone didn't build a network in advance. We all need to expect/plan that one day we will lose our job—our fault or not—and be ready. Develop deep, trusted relationships in your industry or profession. Seek out relationships that are valuable to both sides, and take care of them; talk regularly, share what you're seeing and learning. Be valuable.*
>
> *I have seen experienced people (techs, CEOs) be heads down for so long that they have no one to approach when their job ends. Who would you call today and say, "I'm out, know of anyone that needs my skills?"*
>
> *If you can't name five people on your "call first" list, you must start building your network. By the way, it's not just for you—it's the right thing to do. With a good network, you're valuable to others, which in and of itself is rewarding.*

QA Leader Tracy Olnhausen says:

> *The Omaha, Nebraska job market was pretty small for tech jobs, so I knew someone everywhere and I would call trusted friends to ask about candidate X. Even better, if those people called me first and said, "Mary is going to apply for your positions. She's great," I was already on the candidate's side.*

Ellis says:

> *Yes. My past three jobs have been through: 1. My mother knowing the hiring manager at the first job 2. The daughter of a colleague at the first job working at the second job 3. Someone from the second job being the hiring manager at my third job.*
>
> *(Thanks, Mom.)*

What to Do

If you're interested in a job at a particular company, look up that company on LinkedIn and see if anyone in your network is a 2nd-degree connection with anyone influential at the company. For example, if you've got your eye on a quality assurance job and the company's QA manager is connected to someone in your network, then ask your mutual connection for an introduction, referral, or any information that'd be useful.

Use your network and don't be shy. Are you going to let timidity stand in the way of advancing your career? Imagine yourself a few years from now explaining why you didn't get the job: "Well, the QA manager was a friend of a friend, but I was too scared to ask for an introduction. So, I never got that job, which really sucked because I was unemployed and needed work at the time."

So what if it's a little awkward? Life is often about overcoming our own discomfort. What is the worst thing your mutual friend is going to say? "No, I won't introduce you two because I'm ashamed to know you?" Come on. The worst answer will be, "No." And if you get that answer, at least you know you tried.

Here's a great story from Vita Duncan:

When I was relocating to Arizona, I was applying for jobs and was not getting any action. One Sunday morning I went on LinkedIn and started to message recruiting managers directly (I was looking for a recruiting role). I found one manager who was married to my best friend's neighbor from the "old neighborhood" where I grew up. I explained that I was moving to AZ and wanted a recruiting position. At the end of the email, I asked if she was married to JB. She called me the next day and within a week I had a job offer.

Don't be afraid to name drop!

Key Takeaways

1. Build your network. Now is not too late to start. Get in touch with those you haven't seen or spoken to in a while. Catch up with no ulterior motives.
2. Use your network. Ask for help.
3. Return the favor when you're asked.

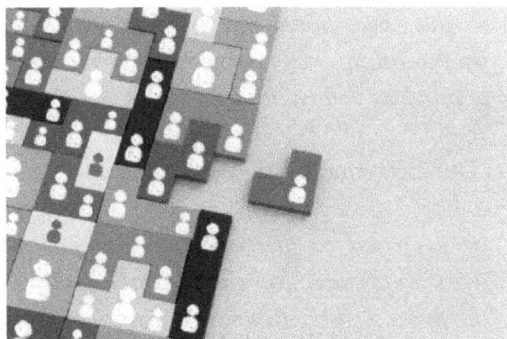

Misconception #14: You Can't Prepare for an Interview

INTERVIEWING IS A skill. Like playing piano, or archery, or running a mile, it takes practice. If you think you're going to waltz into an interview and nail it, you're fooling yourself.

Just a couple years ago, I interviewed an executive who hadn't interviewed for a job in 10-15 years. He completely and totally failed the interview. It was so pathetic. (See the "What to do" section for the story.)

In fact, for my previous role, I was in this weird mood during my job interview and afterward I thought, "Well, that didn't go well." I called the hiring manager and she said, "You're right. It didn't go well." You know what I did? I emailed the interview committee and said, "Could we meet at a restaurant instead and just talk like we're meeting outside of work?" We met at a local restaurant, shared a meal, had some beer, and I got hired. I screwed up my interview because I psyched myself out. But I fixed it by making myself comfortable. I got lucky. You might not. Recruiter Jamie Contino says:

> *If you're working with an external recruiter, they should run you through an interview prep. Listen*

71

to this, take notes and ask questions. They get paid to fill this position and they want this for you as much as you want this for you.

And Vita Duncan reminds us:

Be prepared to give specific examples of your work and be able to walk the interviewer through the process. I try to have at least 5 examples and write out my process before the interview so that I can talk through it.

Ellis has Something to Say

Let's acknowledge that for too many women, calling a hiring manager and asking for a redo off premises is tricky, especially if that hiring manager is a man. More often than not, it's not a big deal, but that's not always the way it goes.

I interviewed with an agency once, and the interview was an oddly intimate lunch with the two male hiring managers. I definitely got a weird, suggestive vibe from both of them, but one more so than the other. I turned down their job offer. Learning that their offices were in converted slaughterhouses that still had hooks in the ceiling didn't help.

But still, calling up a male hiring manager and asking to meet up for drinks is fraught in many cases. Luckily, there are many women hiring managers out there, and requesting to meet for lunch or drinks isn't as weird. But I'd still like to point out to Anthony that not everyone can do it like he can. Do what you're comfortable with, and always listen to your gut.

What to Do

Here's the story of the executive who bombed his interview: He was an experienced technology leader who had probably interviewed 500 people over the past few years, yet the guy could barely answer a question.

He didn't know I'd previously interviewed and hired several people who used to report to him. The feedback from those people was the same: He was disconnected from the day-to-day, he brought in unnecessary changes that slowed work down, and he didn't invest in his team. During his interview, I asked him, "How would you characterize your performance as a leader?" His response was: "I care a lot about my teams and I've done a lot to transform how they work."

I responded, "Do you know that I've hired several people who used to work for you and they all left your team for the same reasons? They told me you were disconnected, you brought in unnecessary changes that negatively affected their performance, and you never invested in their growth."

This is when things fell apart for him.

He responded, "There are definitely some people who would disagree with that. But the feedback you're getting is in response to the fact that our leadership team had no idea what they were doing. They were trying to do too much to change the company. So, they forced me to make changes that the teams didn't like. I was just doing what I was told."

I said, "Seriously? You're applying for a leadership position here and you're telling me that it wasn't your fault that people left your team? You were in your position for over ten years, so you should have had some clout. How do I know you're not going to come here, fail to lead, and then blame leadership because you couldn't get the job done?"

It went downhill from there. At the end of the conversation he said, "You know what? I want to apologize for how I performed in this interview. It's been so many years since I've had to interview for a position that I forgot what it's like to be on this side of the table."

He didn't apologize for blaming leadership, he apologized that he didn't perform better. You might think I'm being a hardass, but when there's literally hundreds of thousands of dollars of salary on the line and millions of dollars in team salaries reporting to that role, you need to be a hardass.

After the interview ended, I conferred with my peers and we all agreed we dodged a bullet.

The upshot? Even people who *think* they're good at interviews can be fooling themselves. It's not until they fail that they realize they're out of practice.

There's a great article with 65 of the most typical questions for job interviews.[4] Shortly after I read that list, I wrote down all the questions and answered as many as I could. It's a good list of questions that's worth revisiting every now and again. The answers will change over time.

The reality is: Most hiring managers ask questions from this list. I guess that's why the article is titled "the most typical questions for job interviews." (Thank you, Captain Obvious.) Unlike most headlines, however, there's no exaggeration happening here.

Human Resources expert Vita Duncan says:

> *Be prepared to answer the question "tell me about yourself", without actually talking about your personal life. You have to be careful that you don't give away something that a manager can use to discriminate against you. Sadly, it happens.*

---

[4] https://www.theladders.com/career-advice/65-common-interview-questions-and-how-to-answer-them

Personally, I err on the side of personal transparency, but I definitely heed Vita's advice. There's no reason to bring up my religious beliefs or my marital status unless I very, *very* strongly feel it's going to benefit me in the interview process. But that's going into the danger zone…let's avoid that for now.

In case it's helpful, here are some of my answers:

Tell me about yourself. I'm a rare combination of creative, technical, and people-oriented. I'm as comfortable defining APIs as I am talking to customers as I am helping my team grow into their next roles. I really enjoy my work and I try to balance my deep technical work with deep creative work. In my spare time, I run a successful YouTube channel and I write books.

What are your strengths? Answer 1: I know how to build high-performance teams. Every team that's worked with me has left in much better shape than when I joined.

Answer 2: I know how to take ambiguous problems, create order, and operationalize them.

Answer 3: I'm always bursting with ideas and I know how to back them up with understanding the work that goes into them.

Answer 4: I have a strong understanding of the business side of the organization. My peers are usually much stronger technicians, but weak on the business side. While I could be more technical, my career path is heading in a direction where I want to have a solid balance of both sides.

Answer 5: I know how to have crucial and difficult conversations because I know how to build very strong relationships. I've worked for years developing my communication skills to such an extent that I once had someone thank me for the way I fired them.

What are your weaknesses? Answer 1: I'm working to improve on putting too much on my plate. It's something I've done since I was a child. My dad would tell me I bite off more than I can chew.

Answer 2: As an introvert, I have to manage how people perceive their interactions with me. I spend a lot of time listening, but that has sometimes come across as being inattentive or not caring.

From CTO and sales executive Marquess Lewis:

> *In my last round of interviews, [I had a call with] the CEO. The CEO call lasted literally 12 minutes. "Tell me about yourself" with the CEO needed to be 60 seconds, max. I spent four to five hours prepping for that 12 minutes.*

Basically, no matter how high you get, you can't escape preparing for an interview.

Key Takeaways

1. Prepare for your interviews. Write out answers to common questions ahead of time, practice and memorize them.
2. Be prepared for an interview with a hardass like Anthony, especially as you climb the ladder.

Interview Listening Tip from Carmen West

Carmen West is the owner and CEO of West Advantage HR Solutions. She has over 25 years of HR leadership experience and a true heart for helping others.

She shared so much wisdom in our conversation about this book that I wanted to include a large portion of it for the benefit of the reader.

Her recommendation for people in interviews is so simple: Listen. When you're asked a question in a job interview, pay attention to what you're saying and help yourself to succeed. Here are her direct words:

> When you're in an interview, **listen to how you're responding.** Many times you can course-correct yourself without asking for feedback. **Listen for the question, take a moment, and answer.** As you're answering, really listen to how you're actually answering the question that was asked. Sometimes you can course-correct to make sure you're giving them the answer they need. Even at the end, if you feel like you weren't able to course-correct, just ask if you gave the info they were looking for.
>
> Be comfortable doing that. It's a pulse check. It's not different from just asking questions and speaking up for yourself. Be comfortable asking yourself questions and know how you're addressing them.
>
> At the end, it's okay to say, "Is there anything else that I can provide that I didn't while I was answering the questions? I want to make sure you have enough information."
>
> Even after the interview, **follow up with a thank you note.** That's really important. Do it in a way that you're asking about that role and the questions they asked and how you answered them. Think about all that for your note because it's reiterating your value and why you feel you're the best person for the role.
>
> Other things I've done after an interview—

*and I don't do this for all of the roles (mostly the jobs I've gotten)—I'll do a **one-page value proposition.** That's the "thank you." The "thank you" is very short and I attach a value proposition that tells a story of who I am and that's really important.*

If you do this and still don't get the role, you usually find out from a standard notice because everything is so systematic. If you're using a recruiter, you have an opportunity to learn more because the good recruiters will reach out directly. That will be an opportunity to show some grace and professionalism.

You can give feedback about the interview to them as well. Be gracious and thankful for the opportunity. It's important, especially for executive search firms. You are being observed, even after you didn't get the role.

When working with a really good executive recruitment firm, you are representing their brand. That's how I look at it, anyway. I'm always going to show up with grace and respect, even if I get a "no."

Misconception #15: You Can't Recreationally Interview

OUR SOCIETY GENERALLY expects monogamy in serious relationships.

It's different when we're talking about work.

Your partner or spouse can't fire you because you wrote a stupid tweet. They can't dock your pay because they aren't making as much money as they expected this year. They can't furlough you. They don't keep a file on you with annual performance review notes.

So, be polyamorous with your work life. Interview for other jobs, even if you have no intention of leaving your current job. It keeps interviewing skills strong and helps you stay aware of the opportunities that are out there. Remember: The best time to look for a new job is when you don't need one.

What to Do

Well, this should be obvious: Apply for jobs even when you don't need one.

You're not in a monogamous relationship with your employer. Heck, how many people have side hustles nowadays? If employer-employee relationships were truly monogamous, no one would be cheating with a side-hustle and no one would be getting fired for trivial, inexplicable reasons.

You don't need to tell anyone you're recreationally interviewing. You don't have to say it in your cover letter. You don't have to tell your manager. You don't have to share with your friends. Just apply for jobs that sound interesting. What's the worst that can happen, you get an offer for something interesting?

There are so many advantages to recreational interviewing.

First, you can test your cover letter and resume writing skills.

Second, you can test your interviewing skills.

Third, you can test your negotiation skills.

Fourth, you can get insight into your market value.

Fifth, you can use the new offer letter as leverage with your current employer or you can say "no, thank you" to the offer and feel like a god.

In the past, I've recreationally interviewed for jobs I had no intention of accepting to get interview practice. Comedians and musicians employ a similar practice. They'll perform under pseudonyms at small clubs to test new material, get paid to rehearse in front of a crowd, and get their act ready to go on the road.

Don't cheat yourself from the opportunity to practice. If your company needs to get rid of you, they will.

You don't owe them anything more than they owe you.

Ellis has Something to Say

I have turned down a number of job offers in my day, and it makes me uncomfortable every single time.

I hate doing it—I feel bad turning it down, like I've wasted a lot of people's time, even if I know that it's the right choice for me.

I hate how disappointed everyone sounds.

I know everyone says that business isn't personal, but I tend to agree when Michael Scott says: "Business is the most personal thing in the world."

This probably holds me back from interviewing recreationally more often.

If you're like me, join me in working to harden our hearts only so far as to unapologetically do what is best for us, because everyone knows it's a rare company that will.

Key Takeaways

1. Apply for jobs even when you aren't looking.
2. Interview for jobs even when you aren't looking.
3. See number 1.
4. Repeat until you retire.

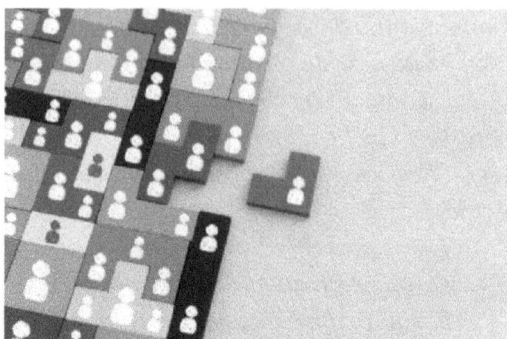

Misconception #16: LinkedIn is Stupid

YOUR OPINION ABOUT LinkedIn is irrelevant. Millions and millions of companies, hiring managers, and plagiaristic, self-indulgent influencer types use it. It is valuable whether you like it or not. Chances are your hiring manager or a recruiter will look you up on LinkedIn the moment they want to look beyond your resume.

LinkedIn is one of the tools of the trade for getting a new job, for finding job applicants and for connecting professionals. Yes, there are aspects of it that are really, really dumb.

You thought I was going to say something to redeem that last sentence, didn't you?

Saying no to LinkedIn is like saying no to a mobile phone.

Is it necessary? Absolutely not.

Did the world get along just fine before the iPhone came out? You betcha.

Do you need to be on LinkedIn to find a job in modern times? Yes.

So, get yourself sorted, log into LinkedIn (if you can even remember your password or which email address you used to sign up), and get your profile up to date. It's the easiest way to passively attract employers and recruiters who might want to hire you.

What to Do

Having a good LinkedIn profile is really important.

In the past week, nearly 500 people have viewed my profile and I've shown up in nearly 200 search results.

Why are people looking at my profile?

I have no idea.

But they're doing it. And if I needed a job, I'd feel pretty good about the fact that half-a-thousand people were learning more about me in the past week.

LinkedIn also has this option to let your network know that you're looking for work. In fact, so many people lost their jobs because of COVID that they now update your profile headshot with a nice little green border that says, "Open to Work." It is a public, visual indicator that a person is looking for a job. If you're unemployed right now and haven't updated your profile, now is the time to do so.

Also follow the hashtag #howcanihelp on LinkedIn. Some people, including hiring managers, are actively seeking people who need a job.

In my book, *Clueless at The Work*, I share a story about my mentor, Marquess Lewis, who said to me, "Every week, I spend 8-10 hours on LinkedIn." I was astonished and said something like, "On purpose?!"

He laughed and said that it is one of the most important tools he uses to stay connected, understand what people are working on, and look for collaborative business opportunities. He told me he's closed several six-figure sales opportunities just by following up with people on LinkedIn and intentionally bumping into them at conferences.

Even if you don't believe me, believe Marquess. He was a C-level exec at a Fortune 100 company in his late thirties. He's a bonafide genius who's summited all the 14,000+ foot peaks in Colorado. I got nothin' on him.

So if you believe anything I have to say in this book, then believe me when I tell you that my mentor thinks you should be on LinkedIn.

Key Takeaways

1. Dedicate time every week to just being on LinkedIn. Like some statuses, connect with people, maybe post some things! Get in that LinkedIn groove.
2. Follow #howcanihelp.
3. Check out *Clueless at The Work* if you're so inclined.

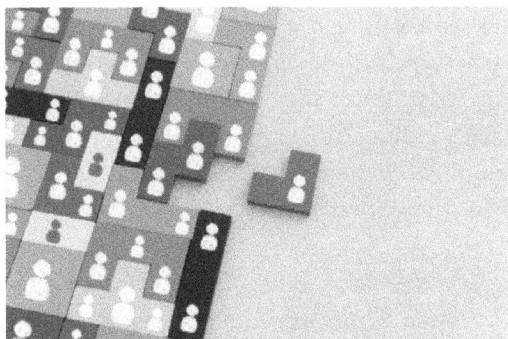

Misconception #17: You Don't Need to Brag

YOU MUST BRAG. This is the reality of selling yourself to an employer. You ever see a real estate listing that says, "Pretty good house. Couple rooms. Old carpet. The kitchen is all right. The walls need new colors. Who knows what the owner was thinking a few years ago."

No. That would be stupid.

If an employer is going to spend the same amount of money as a single family home on your salary over the next few years, you better believe you'll have to brag.

What to Do

Executive coach Peggy Klaus wrote a wonderful and short book called *Brag! The Art of Tooting Your Own Horn Without Blowing It.* It was indispensable to me when I was going through that internal conflict of, "Do I really need to be able to talk about myself? I'm my least favorite person ever."

Without revealing all the details about the book and its strategy, I'll just tell you that Klaus does an exceptional job at explaining why you need to have a personal elevator pitch and a series of facts (AKA a brag bag) from which you can draw to help people understand who you are and what you care about.

You can easily find a couple of great podcast interviews with Peggy (here's my favorite[5]). In these interviews, she helps the hosts turn their own humdrum self-descriptions into exciting and enthusiastic brags. It's amazing!

You might be curious about my own elevator pitch. I've never formally written one, so I'll take a stab:

> *Hi! My name is Anthony Garone and I'm a creative technology leader, musician, and writer.*
>
> *I really got started on my own in 2014 with my YouTube channel, Make Weird Music, where I shine a light on the world's greatest musicians. It's gained a global following of over 10,000 subscribers and connected me in profound ways with most of my musical heroes.*
>
> *I've also volunteered technical and creative services to several startups and university programs, all while working full time in technology and software industries and raising a family of three young children in Arizona. I'm a published author with two books on the market and I have plans for another three.*
>
> *It's a busy life, but I have so much energy and really love the work I do.*

Maybe it's a little long and needs editing, but there's no self-deprecating humor, no sarcasm, and no hint of shame or imposter syndrome.

This is a huge change from where I was several years ago when I couldn't go five minutes in a presentation without cracking a joke about my own incompetence.

---

[5] http://tomyyounger.me/episode-14-bragging-101-with-peggy-klaus/

With a little work and a lot of practice, Peggy Klaus' book can make a world of difference to you and your future.

Key Takeaways

1. Get comfortable with bragging about yourself.
2. Ditch self-deprecation and sarcasm.
3. Write out, hone, and memorize your personal elevator pitch.

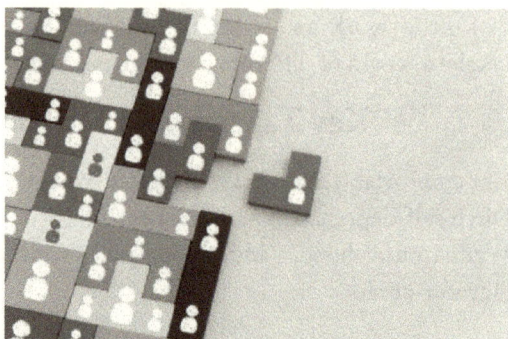

Misconception #18: Working Too Hard is a Weakness

WHEN I ASK applicants, "What are your strengths and weaknesses?" I'm not really looking for actual strengths and weaknesses (though it's nice when I get an honest answer).

I'm looking for self-awareness.

When people tell me their weakness is some BS like, "I work too hard," or, "I care too much," or, "I just give it my all, even to the detriment of myself," all I hear is, "Blah blah blah, I don't know anything about myself."

Or, if you're willing to crack a joke, just reference Michael Scott from The Office and say, "I sing in the shower. Sometimes I spend too much time volunteering. Occasionally I'll hit someone with my car." (You'll still probably have to answer the question, though.)

If you can't speak to your strengths and weaknesses, you cannot inform the hiring manager of the risks and benefits of hiring you.

Remember, you are *selling yourself* to the hiring manager.

The hiring manager doesn't exist to get you *the perfect job* (that you're probably going to quit for some reason you'll convince yourself of in 18-36 months).

The hiring manager needs to be thinking, "If I hire this person, I won't have to worry."

What to Do

There are several ways to find out your strengths and weaknesses. You can take the StrenghtsFinder 2.0 assessment,[6] which will put you into a high-level classification based on your answers. Once you're classified, you can read up on what you probably do well and what you probably do poorly. See if the StrengthsFinder results are relevant and correct for you.

You can also take non-strengths-related tests like the Myers-Briggs test. Sites like 16personalities.com offer free assessments and will upsell you on more detail.

To get more real, though, you should ask your friends, family, and coworkers. A former colleague once wrote, "All your life, you have a sign hanging from your back that says everything about you. Everyone in your life can read it except for you. It's your job to figure out what that sign says." No one's going to be more honest with you than your children, your spouse, your closest friends or your parents.

So, start there.

Like I mentioned earlier, I ask about strengths and weaknesses to see how self-aware the person is. Self-awareness gives me a sense of accountability, honesty, and humility. I care about those qualities when I'm running a team. If my teammate isn't accountable to failure, then someone else is likely to get blamed. If my teammate isn't honest, then I'll likely waste my time chasing down excuses that don't really exist. If my teammate isn't humble, I'll spend a lot of time reconciling that person's ego with a lack of opportunity for the rest of the team.

---

[6]

https://www.gallup.com/cliftonstrengths/en/strengthsfinder.aspx

Another thing I care about is scaling.

When I scale my team, I want to scale its soft skills. I want to scale accountability, honesty, and humility. I want to see more of that throughout the organization. Bringing in someone who doesn't know their strengths and weaknesses can lead to scaling the wrong qualities: blame, excuses, delays, obfuscation, and more.

Knowing your strengths and weaknesses is like saying, "I know what I'm good at, what I'm bad at, and I've thought about it at least enough to have an answer to this question. Here are the ways I will perform well on your team and here are the ways you'll likely need to help me."

Key Takeaways

1. Become more self-aware. Take personality tests if you're into that sort of thing and do a real self assessment.
2. Talk to those who are close to you to get a good gauge on your strengths and weaknesses. Don't get mad when they don't tell you you're imperfect.
3. Demonstrate self awareness in job interviews, even if you're not directly asked to name your strengths and weaknesses.

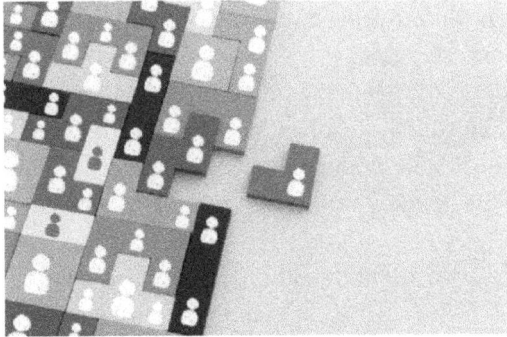

Misconception #19: You Are as Good as You Think

I'M NOT AN unconditional advocate of the Dunning-Kruger theory, but it has some merit. Essentially, the Dunning-Krueger theory says: people who think they're great at something are probably overestimating their capabilities and people who are skeptical about their abilities are probably better than they think.

Most of the people I hire are in the software industry, so I'll give you a software-specific example. People early in their career will often rate themselves on their skills on a scale from 1-10. I have no idea why they do this or who told them it's a good idea. Nevertheless, I often see people say, "I'm 7/10 in JavaScript and 6/10 in CSS." What does that even mean?

What is a 7/10? How are you evaluating that? Is there some sort of exam that people are taking that says, "Yeah, you're a 4?" It makes no sense. Back to the Dunning-Kruger thing, the more senior a person is, the more they realize how little they know.[7] In software, everything changes so rapidly

---

[7] Ellis finds that the more senior someone is, the less they really know. Most VPs are *full of it*. If Anthony ever becomes a VP, I'll remind him of that every chance I get.

that even the most prolific Javascript experts look stuff up on Google *all. the. time.*

You know who should be a 10/10 on applications like Excel, Photoshop, Postman, SalesForce, and other professional software? People who are at the tippity top of the toppity tip top of the market for those apps or the people who write them.

It's good to be humble, and you'll need to brag to get a job, but hiring managers can tell if you know what you're talking about.

You don't need to rate yourself.

You don't need to say, "I think I'm pretty good at Javascript." Bring proof of your work. Talk about the hard problems you've solved. The hiring manager should have enough expertise to grasp whether you're junior, mid-level, or senior.

Bring high-quality problems you've solved, not high-quality numbers on imaginary scales of expertise.

What to Do

First of all, stop rating yourself on your resume—it's not doing you any favors. If you absitively posolutely need to rate yourself, earn a certification or take an industry-standard exam that scores your results.

My friend Brad Westfall has an excellent technical interview testing platform called Questionable.io.[8] His tests are *really hard.* Even the best developers I've interviewed didn't score more than 70% on his tests. Maybe that can be your metric. "I score a 72% on Brad Westfall's ECMAScript 6 test." That's pretty freaking good.

Second, find a way to let your work speak for your capability. If you're early in your career, you may not have

---

[8] https://questionable.io/

much to show. In that case, find a volunteer project you can contribute to and list that on your resume. Let your passion and personal activities speak for your work. Or, find a mentor who can give expert feedback on your skillset. Your mentor can help you characterize your capabilities, especially in preparation for a job interview. Perhaps your mentor can be a reference check for you.

Third, think about why you're rating yourself in the first place. What are you signaling? What are you trying to communicate?

Do you think the hiring manager is going to narrow the choice down to you and one other person and say, "Well, I don't know. This person is a 6.8/10 and interviewed really well, but this other person is a 7.9 and interviewed poorly."

Get real.

The hiring manager is going to pick you or the other person because of a hundred other factors that have nothing to do with self-assigned scores on your resume.

Key Takeaways

1. Stop rating yourself on your resume. Ask yourself if you need to rate yourself in the first place.
2. Use certifications and industry-accepted accreditation to demonstrate your knowledge, especially if you lack the work experience.
3. Let your work speak for your capabilities.

Misconception #20: Your Personal Social Media Account Shouldn't Matter for Professional Stakes

SOMETIMES WHEN THINKING about hiring someone, I'll type their name in a search engine to see what comes up. If their Twitter profile is one of the top results, I might take a look because some people have good, work-related tweets that help inform my search for a good candidate. (Look, I can't account for what Duck Duck Go says is the most important result when I search your name. I type, hit "enter," and I get results. That's how it works.) If it's clear they don't use Twitter for work-related purposes, I'll probably just go back to the search engine results.

If your Twitter is full of hot garbage or mean-spirited commentary, that will color my perception. Even if I keep that bias to myself, I never hire without consulting other team members. Chances are, somebody gon' Google your name. If your search engine results lead my team to salty, unprofessional stuff, it will have an impact on your hireability.

As a fair and (mostly) objective hiring manager, I will do my best to keep everything work-related and try not to let your mean tweets affect my perspective, but I can't account

94

for what my subconscious is going to do and how it will process all that stuff.

Also somewhat related, and thanks to Tracy Olnhausen for pointing this out:

- Don't have a weird or unprofessional email address. TechLeader.69.420@gmail.com is not gonna get you a job.
- Don't have a weird or unprofessional social media handle.
- Don't hand in a resume titled: resume.doc.
  Use a meaningful title like:
  Garone_Resume_SoftwareManager.pdf.

What to Do

When you apply for a mortgage, do you know what the lender does? They look over your bank accounts, all your recent transactions, your income statements, your tax returns, and more. Why? Because they don't want to lend $300,000 to a delinquent.

You know what borrowers do?

They make sure all their accounts look good for two to three months before applying for a loan. They make sure they have a good chunk-o-cash in the bank, their investments are balanced and generally try to look reliable on paper so the bank says, "Okay, sure, we'll lend you a few hundo thou."

I know buying a home is a little more of a life-changing thing than a job, but getting a job is kinda up there.

If you're working on my team, I'd probably end up spending $300,000 on you in two to three years. I'm not gonna look through all your bank statements. My company might do a background check on you. They might do a credit check, too. Or a drug test.

And what might you do? Stay off the poppy seed bagels for a few days. Or maybe you'll run a credit check to make sure everything looks good.

Well, you might want to be proactive with your social media accounts. Either make that stuff private, selectively delete some posts, or use one of those social media tools that auto-deletes posts that are older than a few weeks/months and posts that have profanity.

And if you must have a public, hot garbage social account, don't put it under your own name.

Here's a tip based on feedback from external recruiter Jamie Contino:

- Launch a web browser.
- Start a new private browsing session (Chrome, Safari, and Firefox offer this).
- Search google.com for every variation of your name. Lowercase, uppercase, middlecase (what?!), middle initial, nickname (Bill or Will or William), etc.
- Make sure you check the Images tab as well. Make sure nothing salty shows up that has you in it! You can't control what the other Bill Smiths in the world are doing, but you sure as heck can do something about that New Year's Eve bender you wish you could forget.
- If something shows up, there are options that are beyond the scope of this book. Nevertheless, if it's bad, figure out how to get it off the internet.

Times are tough. Think about how to proactively get ahead of whatever might stand in the way of your next job because it would really suck if your Twitter got in the way of that next job.

Key Takeaways

1. Clean up your social media. Don't let anything embarrassing get in the way of your employment. Also, this doesn't count: "Tweets are my own, not my employer's."
2. Use a professional email address.
3. Search for your name on the web in a private browsing session. See what comes up and take care of anything that risks your reputation.
4. Use social media like your next potential employer might be looking at it, and act accordingly.

Misconception #21: Your Appearance Doesn't Matter

ONE TIME, I interviewed a guy who came to my office from Comicon (a famous and huge comic book-related conference). He had bright blue hair and a very sizable, equally blue beard. I'm not talking blue like the sky or like a peaceful pond. This was the brightest, most neon blue hair I'd ever seen. He had a shirt with a funny meme on it. About 10 minutes into the interview, I had to tell him, "Look, I am doing everything I can to stop myself from laughing. I can't get myself to talk to you without smiling or laughing." He said, "No, I totally get it. I probably shouldn't have shown up with this blue beard and hair. And I probably could have worn a different shirt."

Um, yeah. You could have.

I'm a pretty easy-going guy. I will fight for my team to live as freely as possible. But even I have my limits in the workplace. The guy looked like a walking punchline. How on earth was I expected to take him seriously with extremely blue hair everywhere on his face? (Even his eyebrows were dyed!) Was I being unprofessional by laughing? I don't know, but I couldn't get a grip on the situation and we ended the conversation earlier than either of us expected. Probably because of the blue.

Research shows that…

> *…body language accounts for between 60 to 80% of the impact made around a negotiating table and that people form 60 to 80% of their initial opinion about a person in less than four minutes.*[9]

What impression do you think you'll make if you show up for a job interview with brightly dyed hair, unprofessional clothing, and a casual attitude?

I get that some companies are totally cool with that kind of thing. But outside of some pretty liberal geographies, you're likely to get looks and laughs if you show up dressed like you just came from Comicon.

Appearance matters. Unless you know for certain you're interviewing with a fellow cosplayer, err on the side of professionalism.

Ellis has Something to Say

This is a minefield, because appearance absolutely does matter. A guy can show up in a polo and dark jeans for an interview, but that would be far too casual for most women, both interviewers and interviewees. But you don't want to look too sexy or too dowdy. If you wear heels, will you be taller than the man interviewing you, and will he care? What's the right balance of makeup, especially over Zoom? There's even debate about whether you should wear an engagement ring on a job interview.[10]

---

[9] https://www.nytimes.com/2006/09/24/books/chapters/0924-1st-peas.html

[10] https://www.vogue.com/article/engagement-ring-to-job-

The minefield is even more difficult to navigate if you're a person of color. Do people consider your natural hair unprofessional? Will they be immediately biased if your name reflects non-white culture? Will they even attempt to pronounce it correctly, or will they just designate an anglo-approved nickname for you? Will you look too ethnic? [eyeroll]

It's easy for Anthony to say, "Appearance matters, don't show up with a blue beard." Most women will agonize over outfits for days and crowdsource opinions from trusted friends. Of course you're not going to show up with a blue beard—you're wondering if bare shoulders are too much skin for a Zoom interview.

Of course, women and people of color get hired for jobs, but there are many more things to consider. This narrative is just not as straightforward as it is for Anthony and Bluebeard.

What to Do

You might be thinking, "What's with this discrimination, man? People should be able to look and dress however they feel. It's their right to express themselves."

Okay.

Yes.

You're right.

In a free society, people can and should be able to express themselves however they see fit. But, we're missing a key point: the workplace is not part of a free society. Somebody owns the company. That company has policies that govern

interview-linkedin-essay

language, social presence, methods of working, and more. Those policies often include dress codes.

In a previous role, we had a slide that got shared when clients came to the office to visit. The slide showed what kind of clothing was acceptable for client visits and what wasn't. One item was a man's black tank top with a bare midriff. On the remaining shirt is the word BEEF in big white letters. So, we joked that "BEEF shirts are not allowed in the office.

Why? Because someone else's money was on the line.

If the blue-haired guy had shown up in professional clothing, I might not have laughed. If he had combed his hair or done something to tidy up, I might not have laughed. But he came looking like a fool. I did everything I could to get past my biases. And. I. Couldn't.

Say what you want about other people, how judgmental they are, etc. You're the one who needs the job, not the person on the other side of the desk asking the questions.

Tracy Olnhausen reminds us that how you dress matters, even for virtual meetings:

> *Dress like you would for an in-person interview, even if it is just the waist up. Really, really think about what your webcam will show in your background. You don't want the interview distracted by your unmade bed or clothes laying all over your room. We all like pets, but lock those cuties up until you get the job.*
>
> *We had a really good candidate who got to the final interview and her cat's behind was the star of the show. The candidate just kept laughing about the cat, but would not remove it. End of interview.*
>
> *I had put quite a bit of work into that candidate, so I was disappointed when it ended*

like that.

Try to control what you can—signs on the doorbell so your dogs don't go crazy if Amazon rings it to drop off a package, letting your family know you'll be interviewing for 30 minutes, etc.

And if you do face an interruption, keep calm, handle it the best you can, and don't apologize.

Tracy's right.

I've been on plenty of calls where my own children have come in crying or screaming.

A couple of interruptions are excusable, but if your life seems out of control, that's a bad look.

And external recruiter Jamie Contino offers this tip:

Always over-dress. You don't need a black tie tux or a ball gown, but a nice suit regardless of your gender is always a safe bet. Also, look for a dress code on the company website (many include this under their culture page). And ask the person who is setting up your interview. You can't go wrong asking, "Is there a recommended dress code for this interview?" Just ask.

P.S. This applies to video interviews too.

Ellis has Something to Say

Let's please acknowledge that most workplace dress codes encourage people to dress how white men want us to look.

Sure, at Anthony's workplace they put the bare midriff on a man, but any of us who went to schools with dress codes or work at places with strict dress codes know that most stipulations are geared toward women and how much skin they can show.

There are still companies and professions where skirts and heels are required or very strongly suggested. Some hijabi women are denied their right to wear a headscarf[11] in certain professions. As mentioned above, Black folks, and Black women in particular, are subjected to constant comments about their hair. Michelle Obama, the First Lady, was criticized for baring her shoulders in a portrait.

But what do we do about it?

Well, friends, we have to fight The Man.

But, we also have to get hired. Err on the side of conservative and professional clothing (note: I am not encouraging you to straighten your hair or forgo a hijab), and then get yourself into that organization and try to find allies who will help you fight for change.

It can be exhausting to constantly be an advocate for yourself and others like you to literally just be yourself; but I'm there too, trying to remove burdens for those of us who have to fight to do things others never have to think about.

Key Takeaways

1. Appearance matters. Look professional for any pre-employment interactions.
2. Control your video conferencing environment. It's okay if you face an interruption, but do everything you

---

[11] https://www.aclu.org/other/discrimination-against-muslim-women-fact-sheet

can to ensure a professional and consistent environment.

3. Ask about the dress code before you meet anyone either virtually or in person. Make the best impression possible.

Misconception #22: *You* are the Reason You Can't Get Hired

THIS CHAPTER IS by Ellis. She wrote it in November, 2020.

In September of 2020, I was laid off from my full-time job. It was particularly cruel timing, as my husband had lost his job three months prior. Now, in November of 2020, we both remain unemployed. Our two kids still haven't managed to pull in an income either (blasted child labor laws).

My husband and I are very qualified people, but most of our applications go ignored or are rejected out of hand. We've had a few interviews; I've even made it through multiple rounds of interviews, and every time, still no offer. These are desperate times, made worse by the hopelessness of continual rejection. Michael Scott said it above and he'll say it again: "Business is the most personal thing in the world."

It's a sickening kind of poetry to be working on a book about getting hired when you can't get hired yourself. Why would anyone want to listen to me? I don't know; luckily most of it is by Anthony and he's very in demand.

Here's an excerpt from a text exchange I had with Anthony today. Background: I'd gone through three interviews, all the way up to the CMO. The last step was an interview with the CEO, which they told me they wanted to schedule.

Until they didn't.

Ellis: So that job I was interviewing for, they told me I was their favorite candidate, then they told me they're passing on me...Anthony, wtf. I have a decent resume. I am always over prepared and interview well. I am more than qualified. Just like, wtf.
Anthony: That is really wtf.
Ellis: I don't get it, man. I don't get why I can't get ANYTHING.
Anthony: They didn't tell you anything?
Ellis: I emailed asking for feedback, we'll see if they say anything.
Anthony: Good for you.
Ellis: Anthony, truly, is there something wrong with me? I trust your assessment.
Anthony: My honest answer: I don't know. I don't see it, but I haven't interviewed you.

While it would have been nice to hear an "Ellis I know for a fact that there is nothing wrong with you and these people are unabashed idiots," Anthony's answer is accurate. He's never interviewed me, how would he know?

It is entirely possible that you are superlative at overcoming every misconception in this book and still won't find a job right away. As Anthony said in the beginning, there are so many factors outside of our control. But that is not an easy thing to accept; my family and our future are on the line.

I'd like to remind you (as I am trying so hard to remind myself) that most likely, the fact that you can't find a job is not solely due to any of your defects, learned or inherent. The fact is: there are millions of us out there trying to get a job, any job, and employers have the pick of the litter. They want someone with just the right amount of experience who doesn't have a senior paycheck history? Done. Someone with 10+ years of experience leading teams? No problemo. They are in a great position to sit and wait for their unicorn, because with this market, they probably don't need to wait long.

The corporate world has always been debasing and humiliating, but it stings that much more because these are *unprecedented times* (please, everyone, stop with that terminology. These times are, in fact, precedented). Many of us are already on the brink of desperation if we're not there already.

Here's the bonus misconception: it's not about you, or me. It's just the dehumanizing way of the corporate world. It's a stomach-wrenching convergence of wretchedness. A lot of us are getting left behind.

That's why Anthony and I are here: to do our absolute best to make sure *you're* not left behind.

I'm in the trenches with you, praying that you, I and all of us get out of here soon.

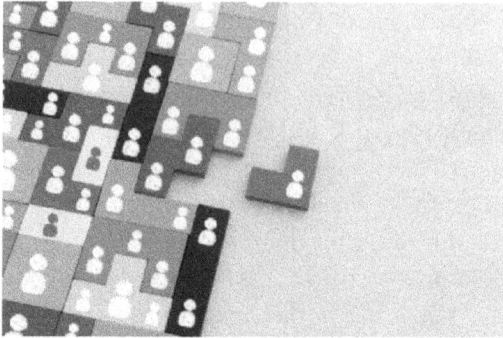

Misconception #23: Salary Website Data Will Get You More Money

I'VE FALLEN FOR this one myself, too. When you want more money, it's easy to believe it's a data problem. "If my manager knew how much everyone else was making in this role, he'd give me a promotion." That ain't the way it works. Data ain't got nothin' to do with it.

The same goes for getting a new job. You find something great, you're excited about the company, then you find out how much (or little) they pay. What a bummer. If you even *get* this job, you'll start at 20% under the median. Yuck!

As a hiring manager, I'll confess: I don't really care what Salary.com or any other website thinks about your salary. Here are the constraints I deal with: budget, availability of talent and market forces. Unless you can pull free money out of thin air, or can prove your pay increase is going to lead to a revenue increase, how do you think I'm going to be able to offer you more money?

Furthermore, how do you think I'm going to be able to justify a budget increase to my boss? Or to the company owner? You think the owner wants to sacrifice a quarterly profit bonus so you can make more money? Think again!

When you're trying to get a new job at a salary that

exceeds the hiring manager's expectations, you need to realize a few things:

- There may not be enough money to pay you that much.
- There may not be budget tolerance to pay you that much.
- The hiring manager/company may not value the position as much as you do.
- The hiring manager may not think you're worth what you're asking.
- The HR salary calculations may be out of alignment with market expectations.
- The salary may be higher than what others are making at that company in the same role.
- Other qualified candidates are asking for less money.

For these and a dozen other reasons, you may not get the salary you're asking. In most cases, it's not about you. Hiring managers often don't have any skin in the game, so it's no significant loss to pay you what you're asking. The hiring manager may have to deal with other problems if you enter the job at your requested salary. You just won't know, even if you ask directly.

One way to get good salary results is to work with an agency, as recruiter Jamie Contino shares:

> *Working with an agency is AWESOME when it comes to salary negotiations. A good agency will tell you what you're worth, a great agency will talk to you about your skill set, ideal career path, preferred management style, and ask what you'd like to earn to make your move. Based on this,*

you'll either be a fit for the client or not. If you're a "lights-out candidate" and above the client's asking price, the agency will work with you to come to a happy medium before presenting your resume.

Some words of wisdom: be upfront with the agency and transparent at all times on your salary expectations. They are there to help and are your best inside track on real salary expectations in your market! Also, remember they get paid to place you in a role, so the more they can champion for you the better. But be aware, if the agency says "this is the max my client can go," believe them. Agencies get compensated based on your salary and trust me, they are out to get you the most they can, but sometimes, we can't work miracles.

Ellis has Something to Say

Most women are quite familiar with the concept that our earnings are frequently not where they should be. I'm a member of an online professional group, and I can't tell you how many posts I've seen where women find out that men in comparable or even more junior roles make more money than they do. And sadly, simply bringing a salary disparity to your manager or employer will not change it.

Whatever you do, try not to throw out the first number when discussing salary, as it greatly weakens your negotiating position. It's really hard, but try. If you're willing to be flexible as we discuss below, you don't want to overshoot and scare a hiring manager off because what you want to make and what they can offer are farther apart than they're comfortable with.

That said, always negotiate. Anthony discusses this more in the What To Do section, but top candidates who negotiate well often at least get something. Re-negotiate even if you think the first offer is fair.

Also, does anyone else think that secrecy around salaries is stupid? Banning employees from disclosing salary—or even just making it a taboo topic—is just a way to ensure that the people who get paid below market salary, or below company median, continue to be underpaid. But that's probably a rant for a different book.

To underline the importance of negotiation, Jeremy Wilson, a CTO, shares this:

I was just offered a job at $192k per year. I negotiated it to $262k with a 2% annual increase and double the equity offered this year during COVID. How? **I proved that hiring me would save them a ton.**

May we all be Jeremy Wilson.

What to Do

Think of sites like Glassdoor and Salary.com as data sources, not salary authorities. It can be *helpful* to know what those sites know, but it is not *convincing*. Having information may bolster your argument for a higher salary, but it is not a golden ticket.

The best way to get a salary you want is to make a

business case for it. It must be compelling. It must be convincing. And it must be backed with enough justification and evidence that every doubt held by the hiring manager disappears. The good news is: writing a business justification isn't different whether you're a new hire or whether you're looking for a raise.

The bad news is you have to write a business justification. That's boring, especially for us creative types. You'll have to use business jargon words like, *return on investment, at the end of the day, amortization,* and *capitalization.* Yuck.

I'll give us both a moment to return to the real world.

Deep breath.

Okay, so a business justification is a fancy way of saying, "Here's why you should make this decision to pay me more. Here's everything you need to know about why it's good and why it could go wrong. It's backed by real data that speaks to any questions or concerns held by you and your management team (as far as I've determined)."

Jeremy Wilson, our above negotiator par excellence, says he sent his justification *before* negotiating the number so that the expectation was set before negotiations commenced.

Whether you deliver the justification in writing, in slides, in person, over lunch, on a boat, with a goat, in the rain, on a train, in the dark, in a tree, in a car...wherever you are. It doesn't matter. The point is that you've written the justification, you've given it thought, you understand how your hiring manager thinks and you know the ins and outs of your argument.

Don't be shy, either.

Doing this kind of work shows that you have initiative, moxie and chutzpah. You've got the mind of a businessperson. You can walk the walk *and* talk the talk. You're a polymath. You're a genius. You're...just trying to get an additional $5,000 a year.

Jeremy Wilson says, "No. You're trying to save the company $15,000 by asking for $5,000."

Salaries are negotiable. If you can't get the salary you want, ask what you need to do in order to get it. See if there's extra work or new responsibilities you can take on, see if work can be delegated to you, see if you can have a more serious discussion in three to six months (and get that in writing).

Just because you got a "no" doesn't mean it's a "never."

I remember walking into my former boss' office sometime in 2007 with my little Salary.com printout. I showed him the bell curve. I showed him how I was on the left side of it and I wanted to be closer to the middle.

He said, "Okay, I get it. But we're not going to do that." We had a good conversation about how all this stuff really works.

It was frustrating and I learned a lot.

Here were my takeaways from that conversation:

- Businesses have budgets.
- Budgets need to be somewhat predictable— predictability is typically the number one reason for business success.
- Businesses will almost never make a drastic change in budget to bump someone's salaries outside of planned budget increases and salary increase windows (annual reviews, promotions, etc.). Jeremy Wilson says he's had to plan these promotions up to a year in advance.
- Salary.com is not a source of truth.
- Just because you have the job doesn't mean you're performing as well as the people higher on the salary bell curve—it's all about value and impact.
- You might have different responsibilities as well—not all jobs with the same titles are created equal.

Example

To get more money, you're going to need something convincing in writing and you're going to need to speak convincingly about it. The situation is a little different if you are looking for a job versus already having a job.

One important note: having an actual job offer in writing from another company is hugely enormously gigantic leverage. If there is another company that is offering you more money *in writing*, that says you are worth that amount to the market. Keep in mind, you need to be willing to show an *actual offer* instead of saying, "Well, this one company is saying they'd pay me 20% more." It needs to be in writing and you need to be willing to accept that other offer if you don't get your way.

Ellis has Something to Say

> *Proceed with caution. You'd better be ready to leave if you use this tactic, because many employers don't take kindly to being leveraged like this. Also, if you stay at your original position because your demands are met, watch your back. You've just given your manager a great excuse for you to be the first to go if cuts come around, i.e. "Anthony isn't loyal or committed to our mission because he's leveraging other offers against us."*

Jeremy Wilson agrees with Ellis:

> *If an employee put me in this position, I would wish them well and immediately look for a replacement. But also that has never happened because I invest deeply in my employees and they know it's not an acceptable move. Trust and*

loyalty are my primary measure of a great employee, so be situationally aware of who you are dealing with.

Recruiter Jamie Contino also doesn't love that scenario:

I advise against taking an offer letter to your current position to leverage more money. Why? You're probably looking to leave for other reasons, not just money. If you go through an entire interview process and get an offer AT THE SALARY YOU WANT, don't choose to stay in your current role. If you have a great manager, you should be able to have career advancement conversations; a threat to leave if you don't get the money you want isn't good business. Besides, if you do get the money you want with a threat of leaving, that tells you that your current employer was undervaluing you.

Additionally, you may burn a bridge with the company you got your new shiny offer from. They might think, "We wasted all this time to interview you just so you could leverage our offer at your current role?" Time is money—don't waste it.

Also, FACT: "80% of candidates who accept a counter offer from their current employer end up leaving within 6 months."

This is a long standing and well proven statistic, feel free to fact check me.

(We fact checked her; she's right.)

If you're negotiating for a new job here's how I'd frame a

requested increase in salary:

Thank you for your serious consideration to hire me at [base salary plus other compensation]. I want you to know that I am very excited to be offered this role and I definitely want to move forward. Based on [market information, another offer, previous salary], I believe my compensation should be [base salary plus other compensation]. Here's why:

- I am an expert in this role and have [number of years of experience, role-specific certifications, other related industry expertise].

- In my competitive analysis, the median salary for this role is $XX,000. Because of my background, I am confident that I will bring much more value to this role by [your justification].

- In addition to my experience, I assure you I will bring [marketing value through your network, potential customers, an aura of attention through my industry following—make sure to note explicitly how you will make the company grow or improve its capability to bring value to customers, employees, and shareholders].

- With this compensation, I can feel good about longer-term employment here. I will feel you've invested in me and I will invest in you.

You could also mention that you are open to other forms of compensation, like bonuses if you can bring in new customers, or a six-month check-in with a financial incentive if you meet performance targets or a promised salary negotiation at the 12-month mark. In one position, I requested a $5,000 minimum annual bonus as long as the company met its profitability targets. These are ways you can guarantee yourself a raise, even if the company wasn't planning on it.

Be sure to document everything you both agreed to in your updated offer letter.

I can't stress this enough.

If you agree to any terms beyond the initial offer, you absolutely must get these terms in your offer letter. There is no gentleman's handshake or professional verbal agreement about this. If your hiring manager quits before your evaluation period is over, the new manager will say, "Well, no one told me about getting you more money. Why would I do that when I'm not doing that for the rest of the team?"

If it's not in writing it has no legacy—it's only wishful thinking.

Ellis has Something to Say

If you get an offer, SAVE YOUR OFFER LETTER. I once got a bonus check that was half what it should have been. I told my manager, who was not the one who hired me, that my bonus percentage was double what she'd told me. She asked for my offer letter, I produced it, and she fixed it immediately. SAVE. YOUR. OFFER. LETTER.

If you are already in a job and you'd like an increase in salary, here's how you can approach it:

1. Create a business justification document similar to the offer letter above.
2. Make it a regular topic in your one-on-one meetings with your boss. Position this as value to customers, employees and shareholders.
3. Recreationally interview and get an offer in your hand.

I've already covered items 1 and 3, so let's talk about 2. In your next one-on-one with your manager, say something like, "I've been thinking a lot about the value I bring to the company and I was wondering how I can grow in this role. Can you give me details on how I might transition into my next opportunity?"

If the boss hems and haws about the answer, you can say, "What would you do if you were me?"

This is a great chance to put the boss in your shoes. He or she is already making more money than you and (most likely) wouldn't want your job. So, they'd start out by thinking about how to not have your current role and salary.

Putting other people in your shoes is one of the most influential ways to create a desired outcome. It also illustrates the things they value most and will have the greatest impact on them.

If even that is a challenge, I would say, "What are three goals I can meet in the next six months that would get me into a better position?" Get those three goals in writing. Put a plan in place for those goals. And make sure you discuss them at every future one-on-one. Track your progress, send weekly emails demonstrating the progress toward those goals, and if you get stuck, ask for your manager's help.

If you have a crappy boss who still won't help, remember this bit of wisdom: people don't leave jobs; they leave managers. If you can't grow at work, then consult and grow through your consultation and use it for evidence. You need evidence.

Ellis has Something to Say

Make sure that you and your manager include your skip-level manager as well. You won't get a promotion if your skip-level manager isn't aware of what's going on and what you're doing.

Jeremy Wilson agrees:

> *This also creates a case study based on working towards these goals and impacting customers, employees and shareholders. Use it as evidence for your boss—or as evidence for your next interview. Show me, don't tell me!*

Key Takeaways

1. Sites like Salary.com may be helpful sources of information, but it is only one piece of information in a grander scheme of things.
2. Write a business case for your salary increase—considering the full context of your employment and employer's concerns.
3. Have a conversation with your boss or hiring manager about how your position is funded, how raises work for the role, and whether there's career path progression available to you.

Jeremy Wilson has some very clear feelings about these takeaways:

> *SHOW ME, DON'T TELL ME! I grow not through salary but by bringing more and more value, which by nature brings more salary. I prove, I document, I demonstrate.*
>
> *My business cases are not written for salary, but for shattering the ceiling above me. I climb the ladder by showing how I directly bring value to customers, employees and shareholders.*

Damn, Jeremy. You're blowing my mind right now.

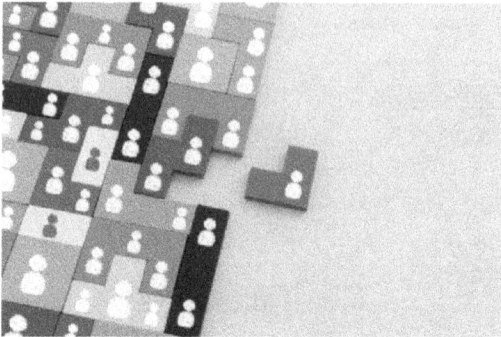

Misconception #24: You're not Good Enough

BEING UNEMPLOYED CAN be a real blow to your self esteem and hating your job can be a real blow to your daily energy.

Looking for a new job can be a soul-sucking exercise in disappointment and a true test of your patience.

All the ingredients for depression are right there. Sooner or later, you might be saying to yourself, "Jeez, I really suck. I can't find a job and no one wants me."

Let me tell you this: the grief you feel in your job situation is probably not your fault.

We wrote this book during the height of the COVID pandemic when tons of people were getting fired, departments were being axed via Zoom calls, and the election season was super painful.

By the time this book is published, COVID will (hopefully) be nearly over, gas prices may be sky high, and Russia may still be attacking Ukraine. Our awareness of uncertainty is very, very high. People in every industry at every seniority level in every corner of the globe are trying to figure life out. As much as it may feel like it, this situation isn't just about you.

Jeremy Wilson advises:

Now is the time to double down and establish more value from what you can offer. Spend your time improving something about yourself, especially in the hard times.

Millions of people are trying to get a job just like you are. Some governmental agencies are incentivizing the job search with tax bonuses or plain ol' cash. The chances of your resume hitting the right queue at the right time to get the attention of the recruiter or hiring manager who can hire you are.

Before the pandemic, I regularly had 200-300 applicants for an open role. Post-pandemic, that number went way up. The greatest, most perfectest applicant in the world could have applied for my position and I just didn't see it because there were a few dozen other qualified candidates for me to look at.

This isn't about whether you're good enough; often things come down to luck of the draw. That's why we made this book—you *will* be drawn, and when you are, you want to be ready in every aspect possible.

What to Do

I know I'm not you and I don't know what you've been through. I don't know your history. I don't know what industry you're in or whether your skills are in demand.

No matter what, negative self talk is just that: negative. It hurts more than helps.

Instead, focus on a few basic facts. The job hunt is often about:

- Luck of the draw, not about having the objectively best application.

- Timing beyond your control.
- The odds of your application being drawn among a pool of hundreds of others.
- How much time the hiring manager has the time this week to look through the pool of applicants.
- Whether the position was opened with an internal promotion in mind.
- Whether an applicant was referred by another employee—relationships matter the most.

There are a hundred reasons why the job hunt isn't working for you, and it's unlikely it is all down to you, your capabilities or how you represent yourself. None of this stuff has to do with your value, ability to get a job, whether your resume is good or whether you wrote enough in your cover letter. Think about this probabilistically. Don't let your self-esteem (or lack thereof) be the scapegoat.

HR executive Carmen West adds:

> There're not hundreds of reasons why the job hunt isn't working for you—there're millions of things. There're so many reasons why the job search is hard.
>
> What I want people to pay more attention to is sometimes the simplest thing: reading over the resume. We tend to lose sight of our value.
>
> When you read over your resume, it should remind you of who you are in terms of your background, your experience, and what you were able to accomplish.
>
> We all need to remind ourselves of that from time to time.
>
> Too often, you're thinking about interview

questions and how you'll answer them, your stories, all that. That's important.

But if you just take the time to revisit your resume and what's there and go down memory lane with yourself, take the time to review the journey that got you to where you are. That will give you the fuel and passion you need to do well at that interview and show up as your authentic self.

So, what do you do? Here's what you do:

1. Invest in self-improvement.
2. Optimize your application using the tips in these pages
3. Apply to as many jobs as you can/want. This is a numbers game.
4. Try not to get desperate. This is not easy, but desperation makes the job hunt harder, and makes it easier to make unwise decisions.
5. As best you can, use your time to reflect positively on yourself. Review your work history and take pride in your achievements. Do some reading about making a new career move. Network to the extent that public health allows. Do constructive things you always meant to do.
6. Stay on top of industry news and trends so you're ready when your interviews inevitably happen.
7. Take breaks. Unemployment, especially when it's against your will, is utterly exhausting. Make sure you take time to rest; don't fall prey to the mindset that you don't deserve free time because you got laid off.
8. NETWORK. Even if we have to return to a pandemic quarantine, you can DoorDash someone food and have a Zoom lunch.

These things make it easier to stave off the doom about falling into an eternally jobless state and keep you productive in healthy ways.

You're going to find another job. Today is a chance to make the day better than yesterday and tomorrow is a chance to be better than today.

Luck favors the prepared. If you follow the tips in this book, you're doing everything you can to make luck work out for you.

Example

For years, I beat myself up—telling myself:

- You are an idiot.
- You're a terrible technologist.
- You'll never get promoted because there's already a protective group of people who want to keep their more senior roles.
- You're clearly not talented enough to do that more senior job.
- You'll never get hired because your resume sucks.

There's a reason my friend Pete set up WrongAsUsual.com to point to my personal website. Thanks, Pete.

There have been several times in my career where I was discouraged, even (and especially) in 2020. The lie I kept telling myself in my corporate gig was: you're too honest and outspoken to be a Vice President and you'll never have what it takes. And then when nothing happened, I told myself: you'd never want to be a VP anyway because they're so removed from the actual work getting done.

You see? It's an unsolvable quandary.

But you know who's telling me all this stuff? It's not my

boss. It's not my peers. It's not anyone who has external bearing on my career and trajectory.

It's me!

I'm the only one telling myself this awful stuff. How do I deal with it? In a variety of ways.

First, I look at all the actual work I'm doing and I think, "Does a loser do all of this work?" The answer is almost always, no.

Second, I look at the fact that I've been employed for more than half my life. Does an idiot have a job for half his life? No.

Third, I think about the fact that no matter what's ever been said about me in a performance review, I've always taken the feedback to heart and worked to resolve it.

Fourth, I look back at the person I was 10 years ago. *THAT* guy was an idiot.

In other words, I turn my perspective around. If I'm the one telling myself all this negative stuff, I'm also the one who can turn that stuff into positive stuff. Or at least neutral stuff.

Also, I go on walks and bike rides and spend time with my kids who are young enough to still believe I'm not an idiot. That works, too.

For whatever it's worth, I even felt like an idiot writing this section.

"They don't need to know this about you. Why are you writing it?"

I'm a human.

Just like you.

We all have these issues, no matter how successful, popular or employed. Realize that your feelings are human and realize that you're the one who's saying the harshest stuff about you.

Jeremy Wilson agrees that it's all mindset:

Just as you are what you eat, you will be what you think. If you don't value yourself, it makes it harder to position yourself as valuable.

Positioning your value starts and ends with you. Your happiness and success in life is based mostly around how you perceive yourself and the world around you.

Key Takeaways

1. Cut the negative self-talk.
2. Look at your situation in a matter-of-fact manner.
3. Remember you are not doomed to failure or eternal unemployment.

Misconception #25: Your Resume Should Live on Your Hard Drive

IF I WERE to go on the internet right now and look up your name, would I find your resume anywhere? If I were a hiring manager (which I am) just looking for smart, talented people to hire (which I'm not), would I come across your name?

If so, why? If not, why not?

What's the best way to make sure people come across your resume?

Think about this in terms of anything else. How would someone know about an upcoming concert? How would anyone know about a discounted service being offered?

Advertising and visibility.

If your resume is sitting in the Documents folder on your hard drive and nowhere else, you are significantly limiting the chances of someone coming across it. And even if you've plastered it online, are you using the terms that allow me to easily find it?

Let's say I need to hire a project manager to help me run ten simultaneous client projects for my side business. What terms might I search for on LinkedIn, Google, Facebook, Twitter, AngelList, or some other platform? Probably things like project manager, concurrent, client-facing, fast-paced, etc.

Are those terms used in your resume? Are they keywords indexed in whatever system I'm searching? Do you know how these platforms work?

Whether you know the answers to these questions is almost immaterial. If your resume does not exist on a website or some place I can find it, your chances of me hiring you are zero.

If you need a job, it's time to maximize your visibility.

What to Do

If you haven't done this already, go to monster.com, careerbuilder.com, angellist.com, linkedin.com, indeed.com and other industry-relevant job board websites and post your resume. Like, right now. Stop reading and go do it.

If you're even slightly web-savvy, create a website for yourself, too. Use a free or low-cost website hosting platform and make something simple. Become find-able. Become search-able.

And when you're done doing all that stuff, go and share with the world that your resume can be found at all these places.

Find ways to exploit these platforms to your advantage.

LinkedIn lets you inform your network that you've changed jobs. They do pretty well publicizing to everyone you know. Create a new job for yourself that says, "Looking for work" as the job title and put your email address in as the company name if you need to.

Go on Facebook and create a Life Event that says, "I'm looking for a job." Facebook loves telling your friend network about life events. Share the URL for your fancy new website.

Post every day saying you're looking for a job. But don't just say, "Hey, I need a job." Actually talk about the kind of job you need. Say something like, "I am currently looking for a job as a project manager. I am very good at running complex projects and writing documentation. You can find out more at [my website, my LinkedIn profile, whatever]." Be specific so the people who know and care about you can target the types of people they reach out to in order to help get you a job.

Even better, try to create human connections every time you post or advertise yourself. Even daily videos of yourself talking about your industry, your profession, and providing evidence as to the value you provide can go a long way to developing connections and creating opportunities.

You need your job search to be visible and you need your capabilities to be more visible. Get out there and market yourself. Remember, there's someone else out there already doing this and they're going to land that job before you do.

Ellis has Something to Say

This is a hard one to implement because there is such a stigma around being unemployed, even though there shouldn't be. But remember, there is no shame in providing for yourself and your family and if telling the world every day that you need a job is going to lead to that provision, well, get at it!

Anthony's response: You'll get over it once you start doing it.

Key Takeaways

1. Be discoverable on the internet.
2. Find ways to market your profile(s) on various platforms.
3. Tell people you need work. Every day. There's a reason companies spend billions of dollars telling you about their hamburgers.

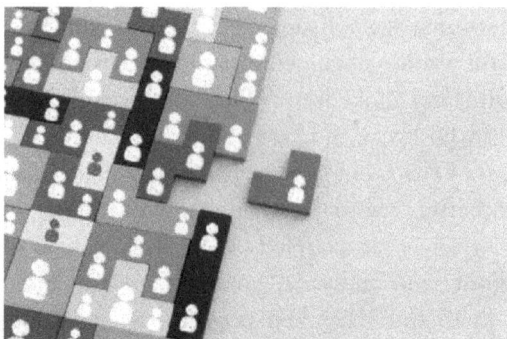

Misconception #26: Using Introversion as an Excuse

BEFORE I START on this one, I want to be clear: introversion is not the same as antisocial or socially anxious.

It means that being around people and talking to them is an energy-draining activity.

Extroverts are people who are energized by being around other people. Introverts and extroverts can be equally social, but an extrovert isn't going to need that down time after a few hours with others.

Back to the subject at hand...

Being an introvert is not an excuse for being unable to find a job. It might be a reason you struggle, but it is overcomable, and if you truly think your personality is standing in your way, you must work to master your shortcomings.

This isn't to say that it's bad to be an introvert, but if you're using it as an excuse, you're likely not going to get far in your job hunt.

We introverts generally hate talking to strangers, especially if we have to do it in a way where we're trying to sell ourselves.

You might tell yourself that the world values extroverts

more than introverts, but introverts have jobs too. (In fact, there are some extroverts out there telling people they're introverts[12] because in certain industries, introverts are perceived to be more thoughtful, intelligent and analytical.)

Stop making excuses and start managing your personality.

My wife and I took these personality tests where a couple dozen of our traits were charted and compared to the general American population. My wife was on the 99.999[th]% of emotional response and I was somewhere around the 16th percentile. We said to the counselor who proctored the test, "Is this good or bad?"

He said something that has changed me ever since:

It's not about being good or bad. It's about managing these aspects of yourselves to be the person you want to be. If your wife needs you to be more emotional, then realize you're going to have to go above and beyond what you feel is normal so that you can meet closer to the middle.

When applying to a job, understand the gaps between who you are and who the employer needs you to be.

What to Do

Listen, I have spent *years* managing my introversion. I used to sit and stare while people talked and a few people said, "Are you listening? You have a robotic look on your face and you haven't moved in 30 seconds." I was like, "Yeah, I was listening. That's why I wasn't moving or doing anything." It turns out that people don't like talking to robots.

12

https://twitter.com/bencasnocha/status/1148657098462359552?s=21

Learn to nod your head, say "yeah," and verbally acknowledge that you hear what someone else is saying.

The same goes for building my network. You think someone as boring as I am just magically builds a network? Heck no! I have to work at it! I have a few chapters about this in my book, *Clueless at The Work*.[13] It takes intention and effort to build a network, especially for introverts. I have to go out of my way to talk to people, to introduce myself and keep enough gas in the tank to keep myself going at parties and networking events.

I spent years being the wallflower. I'd show up at events, talk to one person, and then go home to tell my wife, "Yeah, it wasn't a good event."

Guess whose fault that was?

Mine and mine alone.

It is no one else's responsibility to connect with me. It is my responsibility to connect with them. There are other people who will do this naturally, but many do not. Find pickup lines that work for you and don't creep out other people. Things like, "Hi, my name is Anthony and I work for XYZ company as a technology leader. What do you do?" I mean, these people are *at the networking events*, right? They are there to network. Be the networker. Don't wait for the network to happen, because it won't.

If you'd like to learn more about introversion in the workplace, check out the book *Quiet: The Power of Introverts in a World That Can't Stop Talking* by Susan Cain.[14] A quick search for "introverts" on Amazon yields interesting looking titles. You can probably also find some good podcasts with the

---

[13] https://cluelessatthework.com/
[14]

https://en.wikipedia.org/wiki/Quiet:_The_Power_of_Introverts_in_a_World_That_Can%27t_Stop_Talking same tactic.

And here's some insight from Tracy Olnhausen:

After reading the introvert section, I have two things to add:

1. Now that permanent remote is more prevalent, if you are an introvert (or not) you could talk about having a dedicated workspace, really enjoy work from home for the focus time, not wasting time commuting, etc.

2. Maybe you need to find an extrovert for their perspective. I am somewhere in the middle, but what is it like for an extrovert that really needs people and can't find a job?

Ellis has Something to Say

Being in a pandemic was a blessing and a curse for us introverts. It was a blessing because finally, we got respite from socializing with strangers. It was a curse because we forgot how to socialize with strangers.

Being personable right off the bat, especially in a virtual interview is not easy. You have to practice, and you have to find ways to manage what makes you uneasy. In the first several misconceptions, we talked about the importance of having answers to common questions scripted and memorized. Here, you need to do that, and you need to have coping mechanisms at the ready for social interactions as well.

I'm not a behavioral psychologist or expert by any means, and suggest you do research or talk to a real one, but here are some of my suggestions:

Have a list of small-talk items to talk about. You don't want to start the call on awkward footing. Talking about the weather might be boring and cliché, but it is way better than silence or awkward chuckles. Have something to fill the time from when you say hello to when you jump into formal questions.

Look up your interviewers online before the interview. This can help them not feel like strangers, and also give you context into them and their careers. It could also help create a well of questions to ask that make you look prepared and interested. Win-win.

If it's an online interview, check out your appearance and camera angles before you get on the call. The last thing you want is to spend the interview embarrassed that you can see a pair of underwear on a chair in the background and praying no one notices.

Have all your materials within arm's reach. I like to have my resume, notes and questions I've made about the job description and my research, and a questions and answers document open and readily available. I usually don't need it during the interview, but I feel comforted knowing I don't have to be totally off book and can look if I need to.

It's okay to acknowledge your nerves. I find that most people are understanding if you say, "You know I'm just a bit nervous, what I meant to say was..." It shows you're willing to correct *your mistakes, that you're human, and that you are invested enough in their job to be nervous!*

Example

Real talk: It's only in the last six to eight years that I've felt any sense of confidence.

I used to think being an introvert was a death sentence for a real career. I'd be relegated to screen tans and individual contributor roles because I didn't want to speak up in meetings or because I felt uncomfortable confronting people with difficult information.

Then I changed my mind about life.

I talk a lot about this transformation in *Clueless at The Work*, but I won't make you go buy and read the whole thing right now.

What I had to realize was that the discomforts of being an introvert are not too different from the discomforts of being an extrovert. There're trade-offs with everything.

- **Speaking up and adding value are difficult skills.** Introverts don't like to speak up in meetings, but extroverts are too quick to speak up and can either offer little value with excess words or they make fools of themselves by speaking up too soon.
- **Confrontation is a difficult skill.** Introverts don't like confronting people because talking to people uses up valuable energy and requires recovery time. Extroverts don't like confronting people because difficult conversations come with reputational risk they may not like.
- **Getting promoted is difficult.** Introverts want promotions because they think a lot and process information internally, then they want to act.

Extroverts want promotions because they like working with people to get things done. They like to act, too.

It may feel more difficult being an introvert in the workplace, but the difficulties we face are different but equal to the difficulties extroverts face. It's not easier to be an extrovert, it's just that the costs and risks are further down the path of action, communication, and investment.

By looking at all of my personal criticism over my introversion, I found ways to reframe them so I realized extroverts faced those same problems in a different way. This helped me to see the world differently and helped me to understand that I was too much in my own head. I'd had too much to think and was drunk on it.

It helped me a lot to realize that working is difficult for everyone and not just me.

Key Takeaways

1. Introversion is neither good nor bad, it's a personality factor to manage.
2. Introversion is not an excuse for problems. It's your mindset. Develop a strategy to overcome your the limits of your mindset.
3. Take full responsibility for how you feel.
4. Recognize your introversion and overcome the discomfort of networking. It's difficult for everyone, not just introverts.

Misconception #27: There Are No Jobs for You

THIS IS MELODRAMATIC. You know it's not true. Of course there are jobs for you. You had a job before, you'll have a job again. You just need to shift your perspective or your expectations. Or you need to get your head out of the trough of sorrow.

I hear this kind of stuff from lots of people:

- "I just can't find a job."
- "I've never had it this hard."
- "My industry isn't hiring."
- "The recession killed my company and our competitors."
- "No one needs my skills."

There's only one word for this: excuses.

You must know that someone is out there making money doing exactly what you were doing and they wish they had help—or competition! You might have to strike it out on your own, or you might be able to join a small shop with one or two people. You might have to work for a piece of equity. You might have to go without a salary for a little bit until you get your feet on the ground.

But, what would you be doing otherwise? Sitting around waiting for a job to happen? Hoping you make enough on unemployment?

It will never work out if thinking "there are no jobs for me" is the route you take. Remember, there's always someone out there willing to work a little harder, a little smarter, a little cheaper or enjoy some other competitive disadvantage. To win, you might have to compromise on salary or status. But you need a job. Like, now.

Recruiter Jamie Contino says this:

> *If you fall on hard times, employers like to see you took on work, any kind of work!! Consulting? Food delivery? Part-time nanny? It doesn't matter, put a one liner on your resume saying you've been doing something. It shows responsibility.*
>
> *Also, make sure you know the difference between a job versus a career. Most employers want to know you're in it for the long haul. A career indicates a long-term growth path and that you'd want to find a "home." A job is more transactional—you need it to pay bills, not because you're passionate about the position.*

Ellis has Something to Say

Most of the excuses Anthony listed? They're probably true. Most of them are true for every job-seeker I know. But okay, so they're true.

As mentioned in an earlier chapter, I too was laid off in 2020 and couldn't find formal, full-time employment. So what did I do? I went in full time with my own content marketing service, Edify. I figured, I've always wanted to do things on my own terms, on my own timetable, and I wasn't getting paid anyway, so I might as well try to build something with Anthony while getting paid less than I was making at my full-time gig.

Do what you can to think outside the confining box of corporate America, because it's not like you're doing something else, anyway.

What to Do

I often think of a quote from *Napoleon Dynamite*. Napoleon's brother Kip is lamenting his lack of money and his uncle Rico says, "Might as well do *something* while you're doing *nothing*."

I'm not bringing this up to shame you into making money, but Uncle Rico has a point.

Question some of the basic assumptions:

- Do you need a job or do you need a paycheck? There's a big difference between those two terms.
- Do you need to make as much money as you used to make or can you settle for less?
- Do you need to work full-time or could you get by with a part-time gig?
- Do you need to be a W-2 full-time employee or could you take a three- or six-month contract-to-hire job?
- Could you be an independent contractor in your field? Or a freelancer?
- Are there entrepreneurs in your field? If so, can you call or email them to ask if they have extra work you could take? Most contractors turn down work they can't afford to take.

- Did you corner yourself into a position that is too esoteric?
- Have you reached out to your network to ask if they know of any positions you could fill?
- Are there similar jobs to which you can pivot?
- Is there additional training or a certification you could earn that'll help you get a job?

If thinking about your next steps this way causes anxiety, think about the fact that any disadvantage can be turned into an advantage (that's borrowing from a quote from guitarist Robert Fripp).

Furthermore, you may not have to compromise. You might have to look a little harder or a little differently. There are more job boards than LinkedIn and Indeed. Since everyone's working remotely, companies are changing their hiring policies and allowing applicants from anywhere in the country.

Look beyond your local area, search for Remote in your job location search queries.

This even happened to Jeremy Wilson:

> *I lost my CTO job in early 2020. There were no favorable CTO jobs to apply to, so I created my own CTO jobs by helping CEOs succeed. There was lots of winning in 2020 while being officially unemployed.*
>
> *Now I am a COO and I have never been a COO before—it's all due to mindset, strategy, and tactics. Innovation occurs when you challenge the status quo—there are ways to innovate yourself just like a product.*

Example

When I was in my late teens and early twenties, I wanted to be a world-famous guitarist. While most of my peers had spent their teenage years being cool and hanging out with these people called "friends," I spent a majority of my hours playing guitar, writing and recording music, and making websites on the brand-spankin' new World Wide Web.

In fact, when I was 20, a world-famous guitarist named Steve Vai asked me to come work for him. This was it! This was the chance! Once-in-a-lifetime opportunity! (Spoiler— and in case you couldn't already tell—I did not end up becoming a world-famous guitar player.)

As a young adult, I spent every free hour producing music. I helped friends with their music thinking they would help promote me and my music. That didn't pan out. I shared my music with people on message boards, but that didn't pan out either. Steve even listened to my music and told me how much he enjoyed it. But that didn't lead anywhere, either. My wife said to me, "I may not love any of the music you make, but I love that you make music."

Ouch.

In 2014, at age 32, I basically gave up on my hopes of anyone ever caring about my music. In short: "There's an audience for everyone but me." There were "no jobs" for me. There would be no way I could make money playing music, no matter how good it was, no matter how famous my fans were, no matter how hard I tried.

So I started this website called Make Weird Music[15] and started writing about music I loved. I'd occasionally share my own music, too, because I figured: "If my audience likes these artists, maybe they'll like my music too." Eight years later, I

---

[15] https://makeweirdmusic.com/

have 20,000 subscribers on my YouTube channel and I've gotten more attention on my music than I ever thought possible. Even better, some of my musical heroes perform on some of my songs.

Now my wife says to me, "See? You've found your audience. It took you a long time, but it actually happened."

If you look at all the points I mentioned earlier about questioning basic assumptions, all of them are relevant to my music "career." Thankfully I had computers to fall back on and working in tech is much more lucrative than working in music, but the fact that it took me almost 20 years to find my audience goes to show that it's possible that there is a job out there even for musicians like me who have spent a lifetime trying. That job didn't end up being me performing my own music, but it's an *aspect* of what I do and if I really wanted, I could turn this whole thing into a full-time job.

Key Takeaways

1. Remember, there are more jobs than there are people to fill them.
2. Find compromises you can live with to increase your chances of finding a job or getting paid something.
3. Leverage your network to find opportunity.
4. Keep going. It may take time, but it will happen.
5. Innovate yourself. Innovation = value, value = benefit & impact that is important.

Misconception #28: Your Skills are Timeless

I HAVE A few friends who lost their very high-paying, senior-level jobs in 2020. They were making good money. They have esoteric and special knowledge. They cornered the market with their capabilities and got pigeonholed into a particular position that's very difficult to find on the job market.

There's a risk/reward situation here. Becoming so good at one particular thing makes a person highly valuable. On the other hand, that level of specialization can severely restrict the number of available opportunities.

I once ran a team of highly specialized software developers. They managed and administered a computer system that had been written in the late 1960s in a special programming language that only existed on this platform. Each of these people had high-paying positions and retention bonuses. Once their retention bonus periods were up, they had nowhere to go. There were no jobs. The value of their knowledge had expired.

They had to move on to jobs that paid less and they had years of catching up to do to learn the skills of the modern-day workforce. It was painful to help them transition into more modern roles. They were all really smart and did pretty well, but the way they'd worked as a small team (not to mention their very unique personalities) made their new peers uncomfortable.

Needless to say, reaching the top of whatever it is you do comes with risks. If you're a highly specialized person, you may have to wait for a highly specialized role to become available or find options with new challenges. Either way, if the market isn't looking for your specialized skills and you need money ASAP, you don't have a lot of choices.

Just look at Jeremy Wilson, who spent all of 2020 proving he was more than a CTO. You might think that once you're a CTO, there's nowhere else to go, but Jeremy decided to pivot, showed he could and made it happen.

I said it once and I'll say it again, may we all be Jeremy Wilson.

What to Do

As the job market adjusts to post-COVID circumstances, there are available jobs, but not nearly as many esoteric roles. I recommend looking at jobs and determining the most adjacent type of job that's readily available.

For example, a friend of mine is a very talented assembly language programmer for a large credit card company. He writes code for mainframe computers that have to process credit transactions in milliseconds, a process which happens on proprietary mainframe computers. There aren't many credit card companies out there using this technology. Furthermore, he's the only person under the age of 50 on his small, specialized team. What's a guy like that to do? What should he do if the credit company decides to move to a modern tech platform?

Obviously, computer programming is going to be a highly

sought capability, but my friend knows almost nothing about web development, web-based applications, mobile software development, or any of the skills companies seek right now. But, I bet he could pivot into something similar.

Some believe there are a few skill types: T-Shaped,[16] X-shaped, I-shaped, and others.

Wikipedia says:

> *The vertical bar on the letter T represents the depth of related skills and expertise in a single field, whereas the horizontal bar is the ability to collaborate across disciplines with experts in other areas and to apply knowledge in areas of expertise other than one's own.*

Think about what your skill shape may be. Are you I-shaped—meaning you go very deep in one skill without complementary soft skills? Maybe you're X-shaped—meaning you have deep knowledge that intersects across several domains? This type of self-analysis will aid you in how you might pivot into your next career if you're coming from a top-level role.

Finding ways to pivot are key.

Ellis has Something to Say

Depending on your field, you might need to message proactively if you're looking to deviate from what has been your normal role. My husband has more than a decade of experience in aviation. He once interviewed for a role that was all his skill sets and experience, but in pharmaceutical manufacturing. The reason they didn't hire him? They were worried he'd go back

---

[16] https://en.m.wikipedia.org/wiki/T-shaped_skills

to aviation as soon as he could.

Your cover letter is a great opportunity to say "Given my experience as a [title/industry], I'm looking for my next opportunity to grow and expand my skill set, and [role/industry] interests me because [specific reasons that make you look like an attractive hire]."

Example

The higher and more senior I've become in my career, the harder it has been to find a job.

Earlier, it was easier to jump between positions. Network administration wasn't that different from system administration, which wasn't that different from web application administration.

But now that I'm many years into becoming a senior leader in software development, I can't easily switch over to being a senior leader in network administration. Why? The industry has changed a lot over the years, I haven't kept my network skills up in that time, and I've become specialized.

And even as I looked for jobs where I could recreationally interview, I found myself saying, "Well, I'm clearly not a fit for *that* job. Nor that one. And probably not this other one I just found." What happened to all the opportunity?

If I wanted to become a senior leader in network administration, I'd likely have to take a step down or back in some way. And let's say that my specialization in software engineering leadership increased over the next five to ten years.

Would I be able to find a job outside of software engineering?

I highly doubt it.

The further I've gotten in my career, the more my tunnel vision increased. There's an old saying, "If you have a hammer, everything looks like a nail." Well, the further I've gone in my career, the more nail-like everything looks until I want to find a job.

Recreationally interviewing helped me because I face lower risk when looking at new positions and realize how I'm becoming irrelevant for more positions as I become more specialized.

If needed to find a job today, I'd be looking either at more specialized jobs or I'd be looking for positions that are steps backward in some way. Either lower-level positions in peripheral technical areas or a role that's closer to the individual contributor level.

I might even have to dust off my coding skills and get back to writing code full time.

Key Takeaways

1. Determine if you're specialized so much that you've pigeonholed yourself out of finding a more common job.
2. Look at your skill type: T-shaped, X-shaped, I-shaped, etc. In which direction do you need to stretch?
3. Find ways to pivot what you're great at into something the market needs.

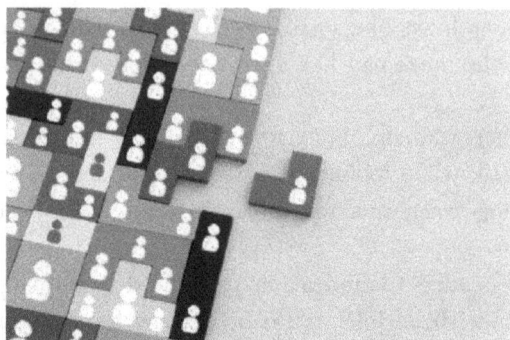

Misconception #29: Short Answers are the Best

PERHAPS COMMUNICATION ISN'T your strong-suit and you're like Taylor, the fictional name for a real person I used to manage.

I'd have conversations with Taylor that went like this:

Me: Hey Taylor, I really like your shirt. It's hard to tell what color it is. Is it green?
Taylor: No.
Me: Oh. Maybe it's brown?
Taylor: No.
Me: Gray?
Taylor: No.
Me: Okay, what color would you say it is?
Taylor: I'd say it's earthy red.

Taylor was a particularly difficult personality and many people found it difficult to work with him. When I spoke to him about this, he seemed puzzled. He told me he thought his communication style was quick, efficient, and precise. While that may accurately describe how he communicated, he wasn't concerned with being effective.

It reminds me of my kids. I'll see them after school and ask, "How was your day today?" Guess what they say. "Good."

They were at school for six hours and "good" is the only thing they have to say.

Not helpful, right?

When we talk about ourselves in our desire to land a new job, some people have barely anything to say about themselves. When a recruiter asks, "Why are you looking for a new job?" They don't want to hear, "Because I need a paycheck to survive." No matter how true that statement is, it's not going to earn you the job.

Recruiter Jamie Contino stresses that answers that are short—but not too short—are good. She estimates that your best bet "is to answer a question in 30 seconds to one minute, then ask 'Would you like more detail?' when appropriate."

You have to find a way to connect your circumstances with their circumstances. Refer to the early misconceptions where we discuss the need for storytelling for your accomplishments.

You need better answers, preferably those that tell the story of who you are, why you're where you are and what you hope to be doing next.

Ellis has Something to Say

The most engaging interviews I've had have always been when I answer more than just the question.

Remember from misconception #6 that hiring managers often don't know what they're doing and many of them will just ask random generic or popular questions without knowing what answers they're looking for.

That's why you answer more than just the question adding context and storytelling—

because you can help the hiring manager realize what they were looking for or hit the nail on the head.

Plus, sharing experiences and circumstances around what sound like simple questions can really help lead you down the path to being a candidate who gets moved to the next stage hands down.

What to Do

When you have the opportunity to talk to anyone who can help you get a job, you need to help them know how to sell you either to themselves (as a hiring manager) or to an employer (as a recruiter). If you are ever asked, "Why are you looking for a job?" Choose from any of the following types of answers:

- My last company eliminated my role due to cost cutting. I really love what I do and I want to get back into the job market to keep my skills current.

- In my current role, I don't feel the kind of support and team-oriented environment I crave to be successful. I want to work with people who want to do well and I want to learn and grow alongside them.

- I'm ready to take the next steps in my career. I've been growing my expertise for the past ten years and I am ready for a more senior position with more responsibility and broader exposure to problems.

Everyone knows you want to get paid, especially if you're unemployed. But most corporate gigs aren't looking for the plain truth. They want to hear that you want to work and, better, you want to work for them. In misconceptions 10 and 11, we talked a little about stretching the truth where necessary. If you honestly cannot connect with a hiring manager or recruiter beyond the need for a paycheck, you limit your chances of getting the role by making it appear that all you care about is money.

As a hiring manager, if I know you only care about getting paid, then why shouldn't I be concerned with you receiving a better offer and leaving as soon as you get it? Think about the impression your attitude leaves. To me, you represent an immediate flight risk.

Another thing I'd forgotten until Vita Duncan reminded me, "Interview burnout happens. Have different questions for each hiring manager based on their role. LinkedIn is your friend when prepping for an interview. Go in with each interview like it's your first."

If you're burnt out on interviews, try to find a new way to engage. As she mentioned, research the hiring manager or other people on the interview panel, see what you can ask them about. Try to escape the burnout/rut you're in.

Here's how Carmen West approaches it:

Part of the problem may be the question itself. I'm more of a conversational person, so I don't like (nor do I do well with) "yes/no" questions. When you get those sorts of questions, you have to elaborate more.

Although the question isn't good, you want them to get to know you. Open up, lean into it, answer the question and give them a little more beyond that. "Sure, let me explain..." kind of thing. Try and turn it into a conversation so it's not just a one-and-done, yes-or-no, question-and-answer approach. It helps you relax more if that's your style. Help them lean into the interviewing process in the right way, so they don't even know you're doing it.

Sometimes you don't recognize a good or bad question. You could be nervous. Don't answer yes or no. Elaborate more and try to open up. Be yourself.

Everyone gets nervous. I will never disqualify a candidate because they're nervous. Give the information the hiring manager needs to make an informed decision.

Ellis has Something to Say

Remember that companies love to pretend their jobs aren't about paychecks, they're about Missions and Passions and Helping Customers Succeed, even as the bigwigs are making dollars hand over fist.

Make sure the interest you express parallels the lies companies and hiring managers tell themselves about work. You can even check out the wording they use on any About Us or Careers/Culture pages on their site and parrot the heck out of it.

Do I sound cynical? Oh, good.

Example

Just this morning, I was sitting outside with my wife. I was playing guitar while she was trying to have a conversation. Unfortunately for her, when I have a guitar in my hands, I get in the zone.

I pretend like I'm able to talk to her while playing guitar, but that's just a lie I tell myself. Guess what happened. Ten minutes of me playing guitar while she's trying to talk led to her saying, "Why are you ignoring me? You keep giving me these short answers and you feel distant and unwilling to talk."

I should have been thinking about outcomes.

The outcome I selfishly wanted was to have a nice morning playing guitar. The outcome I should have cared more about was having a pleasant conversation with my wife for a few minutes—followed by the nice morning playing guitar. There was time for both.

If I were in a job interview situation, the outcome I should want is to get the job offer. Right? The way to do that is to really engage in conversation with whomever is asking me questions and trying to size me up for the role.

When you're in a conversation with an interviewer or a hiring manager, think about the outcome and think about how to get there. If you're on a Zoom call with an interviewer, shut every single other window on your computer so you don't get distracted. Turn off your notifications. Hide your cell phone in another room. Don't let a pop-up message take your mind off the interview or the job search.

Be present. Be focused. Be the person who creates the outcome you need.

Tough Questions to Ask in an Interview

When you're in an interview, it's easy to feel like the interviewers have all the power. It doesn't have to be that way. Here are some tough questions you can ask during your job interview that will flip the script:

- Why is this position open? If it's a backfill, why did the previous person leave the role?
- *If you're feeling really audacious*: Can I speak to that person?
- What are the main reasons I should consider working for you?

- What are the top reasons people have given when leaving the company?
- How would you characterize employee morale? Is it trending upward or downward?
- Are there HR initiatives happening at the company? If so, what are they?
- What do you (the interviewer) love about working here?
- What do you (the interviewer) wish was different about working here?
- If I looked you up on Glassdoor, what would previous employees have said about your company?
- What would be the most helpful work I could complete in my first 90 days?
- What might disappoint you in my first 90 days in this role?
- What is your retention rate for roles in this department?
- How do you invest in and retain your employees?
- Are one-on-one meetings a priority for managers?
- How will my performance be monitored and measured? How frequently will we discuss growth opportunities?
- Tell me about organizational conflict and how it is resolved. Can you give me a recent example?
- How often are employees promoted? Tell me about your recent internal promotions and what a career path looks like for this role.
- Why do *you* work in your role? How did you get there?

And at the end of the interview, be sure to ask: "Is there anything you heard or did not hear that would lead you to not hire me?"

Reword these questions so they fit your style. If you're an avoider of conflict or controversy, find gentler ways to ask these questions.

Key Takeaways

1. Answer questions in ways that get you the job, not in negative ways that improperly express your personality.
2. Employers don't care that you need to get paid. They care that they have a role to fill.
3. Be present and conversational when talking.
4. Don't be robotic. No one likes Mr. Roboto.

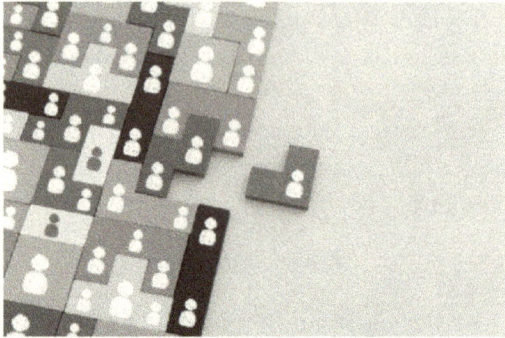

Misconception #30: It Shouldn't Be This Hard to Find a Job!

I HATE TO break it to you, but looking for a job is often a full-time effort. Many, many people looking for work will literally spend four to eight hours per day (sometimes more) looking for a new job.

This is a highly competitive market where tens of millions of people lost their jobs. They need to get back to work. They need to get paid. They need insurance. They need to build their savings.

When there are more people than there are available jobs, you have to increase your chances by applying to as many jobs as possible. And, depending on how badly you need to work, you might consider tailoring your resume and cover letter for your top two or three applications for the day.

This is why there are staffing agencies, recruiting agencies, etc. Jamie Contino advises you try to find a reputable one in your targeted field of expertise.

Finding a job is really, really hard work. There are job postings all over the place. It's hard to know if the job is still available when you're reading the description. Or you'll see the same job posted multiple times, sometimes with different titles because the employer is A/B testing or trying to widen their recruitment net.

Sometimes external recruiters will post a job description on behalf of an employer and won't mention the company name. So you end up asking yourself, "Did I already see this job somewhere else? Did I already apply?"

And there is such a thing as job description fatigue. Reading all that business jargon and requirements nonsense can be exhausting.

Carmen West adds:

> *It shouldn't be this hard! Well, it's easy to say that, but there's so many things—and I hate to say this, but working through COVID has taught me that companies and recruiters and organizations are recognizing that the marketplace offers a lot of choices. It's true for both sides. Companies have a choice and candidates have a choice. I think that's what's taking so long.*
>
> *People are really looking and recognizing the choices they've made and they don't want to repeat missteps in jobs and roles they chose. They're being very picky, very strategic, and employers are doing the same thing.*
>
> *That said, I still believe there are issues with the human factor in terms of recruiting. HR can focus on working in a more efficient and agile way. It doesn't take 20 interviews to determine if someone is the right fit. It just doesn't.*
>
> *Some companies are really recognizing that and streamlining.*
>
> *Others are not.*

What to Do

Like shopping for a car or buying a house, looking for a job can be overwhelming. There are so many jobs and you keep hitting the reload button to see if anything new has popped up in the past hour. Here's what I recommend when searching for a job:

- Set up search agents on LinkedIn, Indeed, CareerBuilder and other major job boards. Have them email you every day with the jobs relevant to your search.

- Create a spreadsheet of jobs that interest you. Create header columns like Job Title, Employer, Salary, Description URL, Did I Apply, Did I Hear Back and How did I find out about this job?

- Track everything you do in the spreadsheet every step of the way. Some job boards let you hide jobs you've already seen and didn't like. Some of them have algorithms that let you give a thumbs-up or thumbs-down if you want to find more jobs like it. Use the tools to make your life easier.

- Look daily on smaller job boards, like Authentic Jobs, We Work Remotely, Craigslist, and others.

- Ask friends and family how they found jobs. Then ask them if they know of jobs you could apply for.

- Find companies you'd like to work for and bookmark their careers page. Search every day.

- Keep a checklist of all the different sites you check every day. Make sure you don't double your work by checking the same board twice or thrice a day.

- Work with multiple recruiters and have them find a job for you. They'll save you a lot of time and energy. They get paid to find you a job.

You need to have a strategy when you're looking for a job. You won't find a job by accident and you can easily and quickly stress yourself out once you start wading.

The most important advice: Take a break several times a day. Your brain can't handle reading so many disparate pieces of poorly written information. It is extremely unlikely that the 10 or 30 or 60 minutes you took off prevented you from finding your next job. Keep a clear head and keep at it.

Key Takeaways

1. Finding a job is a full-time job itself.
2. Organize your job search and keep track of every job to which you've applied.
3. Give yourself a break—this is hard work.

Misconception #31: The Best Time to Find a Job is When You Need One

LIKE MOST PEOPLE, you're probably not watching the real estate market to see what other houses cost just in case you decide to move. You're probably not watching the used and new car markets just in case you decide you need a new car next week. And unless you want to drive yourself absolutely insane, you're probably not checking for stock market updates every day.

So, why search for a job when you don't need it?

Well, a job is different!

It is what enables you to have the house, the car and the investments. Keeping track of the job market is entirely different than watching the real estate market. You're not going to *suddenly lose your house* like you can suddenly lose your job. Think of job reconnaissance work as an insurance policy against ruin. You might be thinking: what's the difference between this and recreational interviewing? Recreational interviewing is more about keeping your interview skills up to snuff, keeping your resume and cover letter relevant, and watching the market.

Looking for a job before you need one is preventative risk management.

For example, hear rumblings about a big re-org that could affect you and your position? Might be time to look for a job just in case. Maybe a new C-level exec is coming in and wants to shake things up? Start looking. Or, perhaps the business is going in a new direction and you're suddenly part of the obsolete, legacy product team? Yeah—you should start looking. The best time to find a new job is not when you need one. The best time to find a job is before you need one.

What to Do

Anything can happen in the COVID-affected job market. In talking with several entrepreneurs, I've heard the following:

- We are hoarding cash in case there's another wave of the pandemic and the government locks everything down again. I can't have my cash sitting in the market where it can disappear overnight.
- I'm thinking of proactively letting some staff go because I need to protect my business. I'll give them heads up—if I can.
- In order to hit our profit targets, we need to lay a bunch of people off. We are in great financial shape, but we need to keep our margins. Eliminating roles makes sense so everyone can get their bonus next year. Gotta keep those stockholders happy.
- The government lockdown forced me to close my business and I had to lay off nearly all of my staff. We won't have customers for at least a month and I can't afford to keep people on payroll.

Business owners run the gamut when it comes to human sensitivity. Some business owners are primarily concerned with staying afloat. Some are willing to pay their employees until there's nothing left to pay them with. Some are susceptible to extreme market changes, which can happen in a pandemic. They just throw their hands in the air and say, "I don't have a choice!"

My advice:

- Keep automated job search agents running at all times.
- Get a weekly summary of all the potential jobs you could apply for. Pay attention to job titles and company names. See if you can discover trends, like whether a specific job title has a lot of jobs hitting the market—or very few.
- Develop relationships with recruiters and ask them what they're seeing in the market. Tell them you'd be interested in talking to an employer who might be interested in hiring you, even if you have no intention of taking the job.
- Follow people in similar positions on Twitter. Ask them what they're seeing. Are they talking about layoffs? Are they concerned? Use the hive mind.
- Build your personal brand today and have it ready the moment you need it.

In strange and uncertain times like these, you cannot be too careful about staying safe and employed.

Key Takeaways

1. The best time to job-search is when you are employed.
2. Use technology to find you a job so you don't have to spend time thinking about it.
3. Befriend good recruiters who know what you're good at and can find you a great job and you just have to show up.

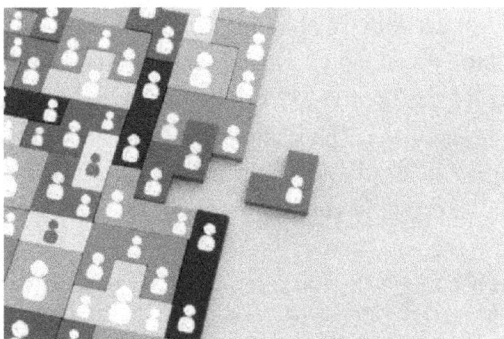

Misconception #32: Everyone on the Hiring Team Will Vote to Hire You

SO, YOU'VE APPLIED for a job, you got through all the initial screening and interview stages, and now you're starting to meet your future peers.

Everyone's smiling, happily introducing themselves and saying that it'll be cool to have you on board. You feel good, you look good, you are communicating and doing other good stuff too.

You talk to the hiring manager later and say, "I'm so excited about this opportunity. How do you think everything went today?" And you get that fateful answer:

> *Most everyone liked you, but there're a couple people on the fence.*

What? Why would they be on the fence? You thought it all went smoothly. Nothing to worry about, right? Oh crap, maybe you made an inappropriate joke. You start thinking about whether you had bad breath. Or whether you looked at someone the wrong way. Or maybe you gave an uncomfortable vibe.

The thing is: you really don't know how other people are

feeling and what they're thinking about you, especially when you're doing everything you can to impress and land the role.

Who are the holdouts? You start thinking about everyone you met. "Now that I think about it, Jesse was a little weird. Something seemed off." Oh crap, maybe Jesse hates you. You think about everything you said to Jesse. Did you say anything? How long were you even in the room together?

Even if you get the job offer, it's likely there were one or two people who didn't want to hire you.

Ellis has Something to Say

I'm quite neurotic and hold a generally low opinion of myself, and I NEVER thought about this before Anthony mentioned it. I will now live in continual paranoia trying to hunt down people who didn't want to hire me.

I recall a time when someone said she voted not to hire me because my pants looked too serious.

I thought she was kidding.
I'm rethinking that.

What to Do

When interviewing for a role a few years ago, I was convinced one guy in particular really hated me. He had such a poker face. I couldn't read him and I couldn't tell if I didn't like him or he didn't like me, or both, or maybe it was just my imagination. "I'm pretty good at reading people," I told myself, "but this guy was a cipher."

Well, when I got the job and started a few weeks later, I ran into that guy. We really hit it off. I said to him, "I was totally convinced you didn't want me in this role." He said, "No way! I thought you were awesome. But, I can't say everyone was on board with hiring you."

My mind was reeling. Not only did I read this guy wrong, but I misread someone else who didn't want to hire me.

This is normal. It's a fact of life that you won't be universally liked, even in a small setting where five or six people decide your fate for the next step of your career.

One interview tip: at the end of the interview when you're asked, "Do you have any questions?" This is a great time to ask, "Is there anything I didn't cover in my answers that you'd like to hear about?" or "What are your concerns with me filling this role?"

See the "Tough Questions to Ask" in our chapter about making conversation.

Example

When you get to the job interview, do the following:

1. Introduce yourself to everyone in the room, whether you're physically or virtually present.
2. Write down everyone's names in the order which they're sitting around you.
3. Write down everyone's job titles, too. If there's a reporting relationship in the room, write that down.
4. Try to mention every person's name in the interview. Keep them present and attentive. Make them feel like you like them.
5. Write down every question you're asked and who asked it. Address that person directly in your answer.
6. When it comes time for you to ask questions, try to think of a question you can ask each person who's interviewing you. Even if it's, "Phil, how long have you been with the company and what do you think it means to be successful in a role like this?" Or, "Susan, how does this role interact with you and what are you

most concerned about with hiring for this position?"
7.   Thank everyone at the end of your interview.
8.   Reflect on who asked what questions and why they asked them.
9.   Consider sending a follow-up email to each person *individually*. You can easily get the contact information from HR or the hiring manager who set up the interview. Mention a question or two each person asked in your follow-up email.

Doing all of the above makes a huge impression on the people who get to vote to hire you. This demonstrates some skills that are universally loved: communication, attentiveness, organization, detail-oriented notes and care.

Even if someone didn't like you, at least they'll respect you.

Key Takeaways

1.   Some people won't like you. But, like the electoral college, you need *enough* votes, not *all* the votes.
2.   It's okay that some people didn't want to hire you.
3.   Don't trust your judgment when you don't know the interviewers.
4.   Ask the interviewer(s) whether there's anything you could have addressed and didn't in the conversation.

Misconception #33: You Start a New Job with a Clean Slate

NEW JOB! NEW opportunity to shine! Right?

Welllllll........

Not necessarily.

When looking at a new job, you might be thinking, "Oh, I can't *wait* to not have these problems anymore." Whether it's a current team member or crummy boss, or the crushing self-defeatism of being unemployed, that new job's gonna come with a whole slew of new problems.

Unfortunately, *you* might be part of that problem.

First, you might be bringing problems and negative behaviors with you. After years of doing the same thing every day, it's all too easy to develop habits. They can be communication habits (Me no talky before coffee...urrrgggghhhh...) or professional habits (Hey team, I re-organized all of our files into folders because I was having a hard time learning your system.). Nevertheless, you may not bring a clean slate with you.

Second, the team you're looking to join might have expectations about whoever enters this role. It's not uncommon to hear in early conversations, "You're filling some big shoes. Jane used to have this job. She was awesome. Let me count the ways…" Or, "We can't wait to hire you. The guy who just left the role totally screwed up the team dynamics and re-organized all our files into folders when he had a hard time navigating our system."

Yikes.

Recruiter Jamie Contino has excellent advice:

> *During an interview with the person that will be your direct superior (and typically when you are in the final stages of the interview process), it makes sense to ask about 30-, 60-, and 90-day expectations for the role. That way you'll know what you're walking into and you'll have a better picture of what everyone expects.*
>
> *I also advise folks that in their first week, they should connect with all business partners or stakeholders they're expected to interact with to understand expectations. It's okay to ask questions, you're new! If you wait until a few months in, asking basic questions about your role can reflect poorly.*

Ellis has Something to Say

Basically, having a new position won't suddenly make your weaknesses disappear. Use some of your time to reflect honestly on things you did in the past that didn't help things.

Do you tend to say "No" too quickly?

I'm guilty of this.

Do you get frustrated that you're drowning in unimportant requests from other people, then come off poorly because they don't have insight into your life and mind and don't understand why you're so frustrated?

Yeah, me too.

This is NOT a put-yourself-down exercise. It's a reflect-honestly exercise. Plus, when you've done this, it will give you fantastic answers to the question "What are your strengths and weaknesses?" (See Misconception #18.) Just make sure to include all the concrete ways you've improved on the weaknesses you bring up.

What to Do

Before you take a job, do everything you can to understand what you're walking into. Always, always, always ask, "Is this a new position or a backfill for someone who left?" If it's a new position, ask why it was created. There's always a story. Companies don't suddenly decide to spend tens of thousands of dollars on some arbitrary new role.

If you're entering a backfill situation, find out what you can about the history of the role and who filled it. Why was the role created? Why did they decide to backfill it? Who was previously in the role? Why did they leave? How did the team perform while the role was open? What would be the most meaningful successes you could bring to the team?

These are simple questions that have almost nothing to do with your capabilities, and they're great ways to show your interest in the role, the company and the team. You want to be a team player, right? What better way than to show up informed, ready to fill in the known gaps, and to share an understanding of the team's problems on day one?

Example

When I got hired for a previous role, I stepped in the shoes of a person who'd only been in the position for a few weeks before he got a new role at Amazon for a boatload of money and stock options.

Everyone understood why he left, but not everyone appreciated that he did it the way he did. The role he filled— and the one I backfilled—was a brand new role to the organization and he abandoned his post shortly after filling it.

Because I followed the skills in this book, I was able to find this out before I started and got a chance to interview the guy in his last days at the company. We connected on LinkedIn and he was able to give me tips for my first day. That was helpful.

When I started in the new role, there was a certain fear in the air that I would also be looking to leave.

So, I made sure to address this in my first meetings with my teams. I wasn't the one who'd left the position quickly, but that didn't absolve me of the fear people had that I would.

If you're walking into a role and don't have a clean slate from day 1, address it quickly, be proactive and find ways to assure your team, peers and management that you are not going to follow in the footsteps of the previous person.

Key Takeaways

1. There's no such thing as starting with a clean slate.
2. Be aware of what baggage you're bringing to the job.
3. Be aware of what baggage the last person had in the job.
4. Be aware of what baggage other people have about the job you're hoping to get.

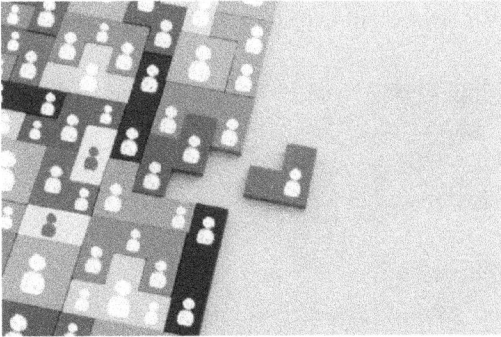

Misconception #34: Writing Isn't Important

WHEN I SPEAK to college students about technology jobs, they're always surprised to hear that many jobs are:

- 50% attending meetings
- 20% reading and writing documentation
- 30% actually doing the thing you were hired to do

The higher you go, the more time you spend in meetings and writing documentation.

I'm using the word 'documentation' loosely to include emails, work tickets, customer call notes, notes that explain your work, meeting summaries with action items, performance reviews, etc. The bigger the company, the more documentation you produce. There are weeks where I spend 80% or more of my time in meetings, 30-40% reading and writing documentation, and another 20% actually doing the work I was hired to do.

Wait, that's quite a bit more than 100%. How does that work? Well, it often amounts to more than 40 hours, but more likely it's multitasking.

We will talk more about multitasking later.

What's important is to note how important it is to be able to write.

Writing is non-trivial for millions of jobs.

One reason your resume and cover letter might need a refresh is that you're not a strong writer. Whether written communication is a big part of your job is inconsequential.

Your boss or your boss's boss is likely doing a lot of documentation.

If you wanna impress your seniors, learn to be a good writer.

What to Do

In 2013, I applied for a job for which I wasn't qualified. I was scheduled for an interview within a couple weeks and was mystified. I even wrote in my cover letter, "I know I'm not qualified for this position, but I'd love to talk with you about your company." When the interview started, I said, "First thing I have to ask is: why did you bring me in? You know I'm not qualified for this job." You know what they said? "Because you knew how to write a sentence."

Shortly after starting my first executive management position, I realized I needed to strengthen my writing game. I went back to Google and typed "how to write a paragraph."

It may seem silly and elementary, but I got *a lot* out of my reading that day. As I got older, I forgot about the importance of what I learned as a child. Topic sentences, supporting points, and transition statements aren't just for junior high school homework.

Relearning the basics of good writing was a game-changer. I spent about six months intentionally crafting every email, every blog post, every performance review, every business proposal—you get the drift. It ingrained good writing habits in me. Not only did I become a better writer, but I could identify weak writing from people reporting to me and

172

people to whom I reported.

Soon I came to believe that writing is one of the keys to my own success. There is no job in my industry that does not benefit from good writing. Good writing leads to clear thinking and an ability to articulate thoughts, ideas, and counter-arguments.

Ellis has Something to Say

As a professional writer, I am really excited for this section. Many, many people think they can write. In reality, more than 90% of them cannot.

You do not have to be a professional writer but you DO have to be fundamentally competent. Here are some things to review, based on common sloppy writing I see a lot:

The structure of a paragraph, as Anthony mentioned above. Please note that paragraphs are not:
One sentence
Multiple unrelated thoughts
Items in multiple paragraphs, like a cover letter, should follow a general order and come together to tell a story. See the example cover letter in Misconception #33.
Paragraph one: Introduction
Paragraphs 2 on: supporting points, each paragraph explaining its each point
Final paragraph: Summary of points + restatement/closing argument
Punctuation. If you know how to use a comma, a period, and a question mark, you're good. Don't understand a semicolon versus a colon or a dash? DON'T USE THEM. Speaking of commas,

please note that commas do not function as a period.

Sentence structure. Subject + verb. If you don't have one of these, you don't have a sentence.

If you use a fancy word, make sure you actually know what it means. I can't tell you how often I Google words just to make sure I'm using them in the correct manner.

Key Takeaways

1. Writing is important.
2. Writing is important.
3. Writing is important.
4. Learn how to write. Re-learn if you have to.
5. Spend time practicing.

Misconception #35: You Don't Need a Cover Letter

COVER LETTERS ARE tricky. Are they important? Who reads them? Do they get read before the resume? After? Why do they even exist?

The answer to all these questions is: nobody knows.

The reasons are many. Even in my own hiring, there have been roles for which I read cover letters and other roles for which I've ignored them. My own inconsistency is not the basis for this whole section. Inconsistency is universal when it comes to a cover letter. As a hiring manager, we had a prompt for all job applicants: "What makes you unique?" The answer to that question was often the gateway to reading someone's resume (and cover letter—sometimes).

I've asked other hiring managers and their answers are mixed.

Some read them, some don't.

Sometimes the Applicant Tracking System (the software that collects and stores job postings and applications) allows an applicant to submit a cover letter. Sometimes in PDF format, sometimes as plain text. Sometimes the software doesn't allow it. Or the HR department disabled that feature. It's really tough to pin down.

One answer I got on LinkedIn from an external recruiter:

> *From our experience, it seems to depend on the recruiter's preference for a cover letter. More often than not, the cover letter is used as a candidate differentiator.*
>
> *For example, the recruiter may ask for a particular word/sentence to be used in the cover letter which measures a candidate's ability to follow instructions and their interest in the opportunity.*
>
> *I'm not sure cover letters are read in their entirety, but likely do serve a purpose.*

Here's how Jeremy Wilson approaches cover letters:

> *As a hiring manager, I almost never read the cover letter. I quickly scan the resume for job description fit and if I think there could be a match, then I might look at the cover letter, but only if I plan to interview them.*

And recruiter Jamie Contino's feelings toward cover letters for those in technical professions:

> *Based on my ten years of technology staffing experience, you don't need a cover letter. When it comes to technical positions, the manager is looking for your tech stack, projects you've worked on and coding samples.*
>
> *Make sure your Github (if you're a developer) and LinkedIn profile are on point and include these on your resume. They will speak louder than a cover letter.*

What to Do

Obviously, the importance of cover letters is inconclusive.

So, we recommend you write one anyway.

I'll often click the "Apply" button just to see if it's possible to submit one. If the opportunity is there, I'll write one. Here's one I wrote this year while recreationally interviewing:

Hello,

Thanks for taking the time to review my application for the VP of Engineering role. I love your company's mission of helping people have better lives through personal finance. Your company is doing awesome work in the industry and I'm excited to see if we can work together.

As an engineering leader, I care strongly about developing high-performance teams and helping them to improve and consistently deliver software. The problems I typically solve are technically ambiguous with loose team structure. I am often called in to turn a problem into a self-running solution.

My areas of experience truly are cross-functional: product, marketing, sales, design, and more. I led and grew a successful design and software agency for five years before I joined a startup to help it get acquired less than a year later. I understand rapid growth, scalability and global software delivery. In 2019, I helped scale our engineering team from 15 people to 90+ in less than a year, all while delivering a brand new product to market.

I am a strategic leader with excellent communication skills. My first book, *Clueless at The Work*, is largely about becoming a better communicator and business professional while recognizing the need for humility and self-awareness. It's important to plan for the future, act on that plan and know when to deviate from the plan.

I'm very familiar with leading remote teams across many time zones and nations, especially in highly dynamic situations with constantly-shifting priorities, growing teams and competitive landscapes. I'm all about cross-functional teams, working with product leaders, and helping technologists get better at what they do. It would be awesome to talk to you about this position. Please call me at XXX-XXXX or email me at anthony@edifycontent.com.

Thanks again for taking the time to read my application.

You can see I incorporated their company's mission statement in my letter, I used terminology and sentence structure directly from the job description, and directly addressed several points in their requirements about needing to be a cross-functional leader.

They emphasized the need for clear communication in their JD, so I responded by mentioning my book.

Very often, job descriptions give you everything you need for a cover letter that speaks directly to the hiring manager. Just look for key phrases that you can copy and paste into your cover letter and you're good to go.

Ellis has Something to Say

If you're coming here looking for commentary on the writing, woohoo! Notice how each of Anthony's paragraphs address separate but thematically related topics. Then he brings it all together with his closing statement of giving him a call.

Nice work, Anthony!

Key Takeaways

1. If there's an opportunity to submit a cover letter, then do it.
2. Align your cover letter with the JD.
3. Accept that it's possible no one will read your cover letter.

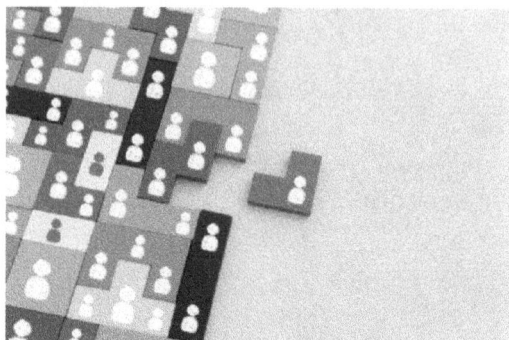

Misconception #36: External Recruiters Want You to Get Hired

ALL RIGHT, ALL right. I'll admit this misconception is a little unfair, but only *a little*.

Why? Many firms give credence to "recruiter" being a dirty word.

Ask The Headhunter points out several reasons: [17]

- *The number one problem is that recruiting is now wholly automated. Both the HR profession and independent recruiters don't really recruit. [...] But, show me 1,000 recruiters and I'll show you 999 lazy keypunchers who are terrified to talk to anyone, and content to get paid for diddling their keyboards.*

- *The other biggest problem is that the cost of entry into the recruiting business is virtually zero. Anybody with an internet connection and a cell phone can play. The automation thus allows a proliferation of drive-by recruiters who run over job applicants while scratching their lottery tickets.*

---

[17] https://www.asktheheadhunter.com/7300/why-do-recruiters-suck-so-bad

I'll add my own reasons:

- I've had recruiters re-recruit people I've hired from them just a few months ago.
- They're expensive. Many of them demand up to 30% of the base salary for their service. If I hire someone at a $100,000 base salary, I have to pay the recruiter $30,000.
- I recently had a recruiter recruiting me and several of my peers *at the same time for the same job*. I don't want to compete against my own team members!
- Some recruiters don't care about the job, the employer, or the applicant. They care about one thing: getting paid.

I have long-term relationships with excellent recruiters who are in it for all the right reasons. They earn their paycheck, they are flexible, and they're good people who value long-term relationships. I've interviewed a couple of them for my podcast and they all talked about why recruiters have a bad name.

If a recruiter reaches out to you for a job with an anomalously high base salary, that means they're trying to reel you in and they want to negotiate the highest salary so they max out their 30%. You'll never hear from them again after they place you in the role.

We asked recruiter Jamie Contino for her perspective:

> *External recruiters have a bad reputation because there are a lot of inexperienced noobs out there just looking to make a quick buck. Tenure is key when screening for a recruiter to work with. Not to say newbies are all bad, but the company they*

work for should have a senior leadership team with strong tenure.

Ask the recruiter about market intel and see how they respond. They should be well versed in the roles they are recruiting on. A great recruiter will tell you, "I don't know, let me find out for you," and will actually follow up. They will help guide you through the interview process with interview preps, interview debriefs, and regular check-ins throughout the interview process. They will build a relationship with you!

What to Do

I mentioned that I was competing with two of my own team members for a position because we were all recruited by the same person. What ended up happening was a recruiter reached out to all three of us separately for a position at the same company. She was intentionally trying to recruit people from under my CTO because she knew the CTO hired strong people.

She didn't know that my peers and I had tight connections and would tell each other about potential job opportunities. When we all found out we were competing for the same position, I called the recruiter and said that it was unethical to pit us all against each other. She said, "Well, the job titles are the same, but there are three different jobs." I said, "What if we all get the jobs? Are we all going to resign at the same time and ditch our teams? How would that look?"

It was unbelievable that she couldn't see the ethical quandary in this situation. Her response was, "Well, if you never want to talk to me again, I won't hold that against you."

Um, drama queen.

So, how do you find a recruiter who's worth working with? The answer isn't so easy. But I assure you it's worth it.

First of all, look for a place that's been in business for 10+ years. Check out their CEO on LinkedIn and see what they post, whether they get engagement and whether they're positive forces in their community.

For example, Sharon Bondurant is a friend who founded of The Finders, a tech recruiting firm she started as a single mother with nothing more than a phone and a computer in her apartment about 20 years ago. Now it's a multi-million dollar agency. Sharon regularly speaks at community events and on podcasts, posts encouraging videos about her personal growth and learning opportunities, and has long-term relationships with many of her followers.

Second, look at how many jobs the recruiting agency is representing. You don't want an agency that has hundreds of jobs and dozens of recruiters. That's a sign of an agency that's gotten too big and is probably run more like a business than a relationship-driven service.

Third, look at the size of the team. If there are fewer than 20 recruiters at the company, it's a pretty small team and they're likely focused on being a well-run shop that depends on long-term relationships.

Fourth, ask for a referral. See if you can talk to someone they recently placed and ask questions about the experience. If the agency won't give you a referral, you probably don't want to work with them.

Jamie Contino is onboard with referrals:

If someone landed a job through a recruiter, ask who and reach out. You should also expect a great recruiter to coach you and be a feedback machine. And then take their advice, they know the client best. That's why the client is paying a fee to the agency. It's their job to know the client and find the right fit.

Key Takeaways

1. Not all external recruiters are bad, but many are.
2. Find a good one and build a good relationship.
3. Not all employers want to work with recruiters, so that may color your chances of getting hired through one.

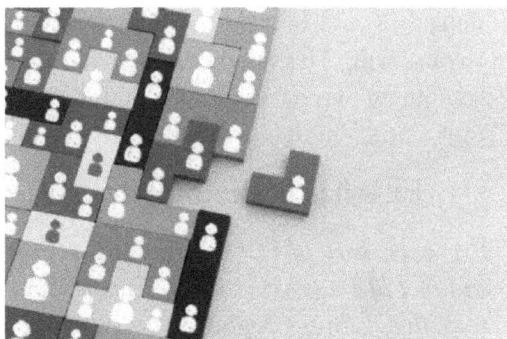

Misconception #37: You're Joining a Family!

THIS ONE I find pretty egregious.

A healthy, functional family does not demote, fire, sue, or put other family members on Performance Improvement Plans.

It does not have a rotating cast of members, nor does it have reviews on Glassdoor.com.

There are a hundred reasons why a company is not a family.

It's one thing to have a family-like atmosphere with tight-knit relationships and real consideration for the human beings in each role at a company. It's another thing to say, "We are a family." The moment a corporate leader says you're part of a family is the moment that leader is introducing bias and leverage into their relationships with their teams. That is a problem and a red flag should appear in your mind.

If you have a problem with your manager, are you going to go tattle on them to Mommy, who happens to be the Chief Human Resources Officer? What if Daddy-the-CEO tells to get a project done or you lose your job next week? This is effed up.

Even if you feel like you have family at work, remember

that it's unlikely you'll be retiring there and perhaps equally unlikely anyone will. This family can sue you into oblivion if you do something wrong or if they want to make you a scapegoat for a problem they created.

Ellis has Something to Say

I've been part of teams where we all get along and feel like a great group of friends/family. But something always happens you would never go along with if you were actually friends/family, but you have to since you're not actually family. And then it hurts more.

I've also worked places where executives and middle management were actual family members to some degree. It sucks for everyone who isn't part of the literal family.

Make friends, but as best you can, don't get sucked into the 'family' nonsense. It's just one way they guilt you into overstepping boundaries.

What to Do

You might hear "we are a family" at smaller companies and that has a completely different connotation than hearing it from a C-level executive at a company with hundreds or thousands of employees.

It's not a cardinal sin but rather an indicator of the personality and perspective of the executive. If they see their staff as family, what does that mean? How and why are they saying it? How might they treat you when there's a problem? Are you still family or was that just for show?

In situations like this, I refer to insightful books to help me. LinkedIn founder/chairman Reid Hoffman co-authored a book called *The Alliance: Managing Talent in the Networked*

Age.[18] This book has a lot to say about the family angle. He recommends a much more humane employer/employee relationship. I've found *The Alliance* to be so helpful, I've given dozens of copies away to my managers and employees.

What I love about *The Alliance* is the recommendation that managers lead one-on-one conversations like this:

> *The reality is that you're probably not going to retire here and neither am I. It's my job to help prepare you for your next role and it's your job to help me and my team succeed. We can make this work for both of us by committing to trust each other, investing in our growth and relationship, and offering each other the right to first conversation. If I ever have a problem with you, I am coming to you first instead of talking to a dozen other people. I'm asking you to do the same.*

By treating each other as adults, it can fix the whole family problem. But what can you, as an applicant or employee, do?

Aside from recommending Hoffman's book to your current or future team, here are a couple of options:

- When interviewing for a position, ask questions about whether people have gotten promoted in recent years. How are promotions identified? How are employees recognized? How are HR problems handled? What if there's an expectation or performance mismatch? Would your hiring manager or team work closely with you to fix it?
- If you get a chance to interview with team members or

---

[18] http://www.theallianceframework.com/

peers (and you should always ask to whether or not they plan to), ask questions related to ones I just mentioned. How are high-performers rewarded? How are low-performers managed? Does the company promote from within or hire externally? Does the boss invest in the team?

- If you get to talk to a Human Resources representative at the company, ask about career growth opportunities. Do they provide training and conference budgets? How about access to tools like LinkedIn Learning or Pluralsight? Do employees even have the time to use those tools or are they so swamped with work they can't?

Answers to these questions will help you understand how truly familial the environment is and whether people are treated humanely.

Here's what Carmen West has to say:

> As a leader, I don't use the word "family." For me, being a servant leader, candidates would be joining a team where we do care about each other. That means respecting each other. It also means that a leader will not always agree with you, but they will always be respectful in their approach and style whether the message is good or bad.
>
> That is what you want.
>
> People who go through life and think everything should be given to them will struggle. They won't know what to do when things don't go their way, even if a caring leader is doing their best. There will always be that confrontation.
>
> I wouldn't use the word "family" for that.

We want to build cultures and teams and individuals to show up every day, to care about the work, the mission, vision, values, and drive for resolve. But we do it in a way that they're being the best that they can be.

The goal should be adding value.

I'm a leader in HR, but I'm also an individual. I show up authentically as a person first and foremost. The HR part comes after. My family is truly outside of work.

I have a respectful style at work, but my coworkers are not my family.

Key Takeaways

1. You are not joining a family. You are joining a company. They may treat each other like family, but they (usually) aren't family.
2. Check out *The Alliance*.
3. Use the job interview to understand what the employer values and how you'll be treated if you get the job.

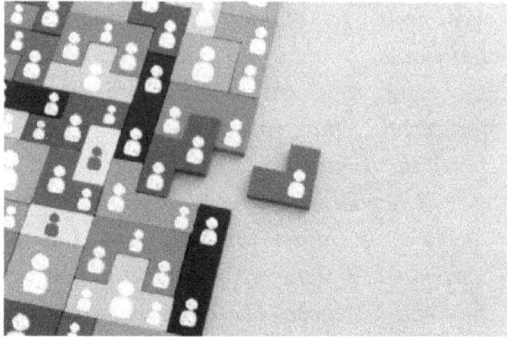

Misconception #38: You're too Old to Change Careers

I'VE COUNSELED SEVERAL people twice my age looking to change careers. I've been an advisor to several dev bootcamp programs, multiple community colleges and spent five years as the chairman of the industry advisory board for the Graphic Information Technology program at Arizona State University. I've spoken to a very wide variety of people looking to get out of their current industry and start working in technology.

The beautiful thing about technology as a career is the low barrier to entry. Anyone can take a variety of free online courses and become a software developer, network administrator, Linux expert, or something else. It's fantastic. However, there are real biases at play.

Ageism is a serious problem for people who've spent 20 or 30 years advancing their career in one industry and want to shift elsewhere, especially for women. No matter how many anti-discrimination programs or laws are in place, it can be difficult to convince a hiring manager in their 20s or 30s that someone twice their age is ready for a new career. Ageism is one of those forms of discrimination that flies under the radar.

But let me tell you, if you're considering a shift into

another career, there are absolutely companies and hiring managers who would love to have you. In my anecdotal research, I've spoken with dozens of hiring managers who see the value in hiring a person who's worked professionally for decades, even in junior positions. Chances are experienced professionals in any industry have dealt with team members not showing up, they understand business problems, they are better connected to customer needs, and are better at prioritizing what's important. No matter the industry, experience is experience and last time I checked, humans work in every industry. Solving human problems is hard. Learning technical or specialized skills is much easier.

As Nassim Taleb once said: "Any idiot can be intelligent."

What to Do

If you're more advanced in your career, you have likely faced ageism. Remember that ageism is discrimination, even if it's positive discrimination. If I were to hire an older person for a senior role because I felt their salt-and-pepper hair gave me a sense of respect for their wisdom, I'm still discriminating. The job should be offered based on the merits and capabilities of the applicant with as little discrimination as possible.

But let's face it, we're human.

Even hiring processes that anonymize applicants have their forms of bias. It's inevitable. We're not hiring based on artificial intelligence analysis with randomized control trials. We're hiring based on how we feel about a candidate. It's not like we can work with an applicant for a couple weeks and then decide, "Okay, I'm good to hire this person." We have to use our gut reactions, professional instincts, and a psychic sense of the future.

So, how do we counter ageism? My personal recommendation, and Ellis may disagree with me, is to play to the biases. Lean on those years of experience. Make it clear you are an established candidate with a proven track record of success. You have encountered and solved all manner of problems faced by businesses. Find ways of aligning your work experience with what the hiring manager is seeking.

Just like every other piece of advice we offer in this book, you should find a way to sell yourself, make yourself seem awesome, and play to your advantages. You want to create a compelling case to be hired. If you have 20 or 30 years of experience, use it. If you've solved hard problems in your career, share them. I know several people who've done this and they start in lower-level roles only to find themselves quickly rising into managerial positions because they have developed a universal, problem-solving instinct that's helpful to any business.

Ellis has Something to Say

Not to harp on the "Not for women thing," but...well, leaning on your years of experience doesn't work as well if you're a woman. I'm still in my 30s, but my mother, a highly-competent professional in her early 60s, definitely feels the effects of ageism. She has found so often that companies aren't looking for the establishment that comes with a woman who has been in her field for 40 years. Why? Well, they'd have to pay her more, but also, let's be real about the fact that society in general values women less the more they age. And since society is made up of actual people, that can make getting a well-paying job a real hardship for older women.

I'm sure older men suffer ageism as well, but benefit from the perception differences between a 60 year-old man and a 60 year-old woman. Gray hair is perceived as distinguished on the former, and haggard on the latter.

That doesn't mean you shouldn't take Anthony's advice if you're an older job seeker, you should. But also know that I see you, and you are not imagining this bias. There's a reason the Age Discrimination in Employment Act exists, and it's not because companies are falling over themselves to hire people they perceive to be too close to retirement. But it may take you longer to find something than it takes the average whippersnapper. On behalf of young-ish people, I apologize.

Key Takeaways

1. Age is not a factor in your capability, but it is part of a greater bias called ageism.
2. Leverage your age and experience—these are advantages.
3. People are going to play to their biases no matter what.
4. If you lost your job this year, see if your former employer is offering placement or training services as part of your severance package.

Misconception #39: You Can Walk Into the Interview and Ace It

IN MISCONCEPTION #13, I showed that it's wrong to believe you can't prepare for an interview and shared the story of an executive I interviewed who totally failed his interview. Well, misconception #37 is a little different. Let's talk about the other end of that spectrum.

Let's say you've prepared for the interview, you've memorized the job description, you've read every blog post on the company's website and you've even stalked a few of their employees on LinkedIn. You *really* want this job. You're ready for all your hard work to pay off.

As you may already know, interviews are a high-risk and unpredictable hotbed of personalities, mood swings, biases and uncontrollable circumstances. I once interviewed for a position and one of the two interviewers showed up 20 minutes late because he woke up late. It was 9:20 AM (eyeroll) when he showed up. I've conducted interviews where one of my panelists decided to go all macho with his line of questioning and I couldn't keep him under control. I've had interviewees show up late because of a car accident on the freeway and they're completely frazzled by the time they get to me.

You never know what you're going to encounter on the

way to (or in the middle of) an interview. I've interviewed after too many glasses of iced tea and had to pee in a major way about halfway through the interview. The whole time I'm thinking, "Should I keep answering questions or tell these people my bladder is going to explode? Is it worth the five minutes we lose? What will they think about me leaving? Will that hurt my chances of getting the job?"

You could find that one of your interviewers was your ex-wife's best friend, or maybe an old boyfriend from college. You could be interviewing with a person who just lost a family member from COVID. You could be interviewing with someone who is drunk or high (I've had it happen). You could be interviewing at a company that allows pets in the office and the dog is really, really interested in sniffing you intimately (I've seen that happen, too).

Anything can knock you off your game. Be prepared to be unprepared.

What to Do

While you can't control whatever is going to happen in real life, you can be prepared to be unprepared. One mantra that has helped me is: "Relax. Nothing is under control." And isn't control what this whole misconception is about anyway?

You're not under control, no matter how much preparation you've done. What if you've memorized your sixty-second elevator pitch and the interviewer's cell phone rings in the middle of it? Or, since so many of us are working from home, what if someone's kid interrupts your flow?

This stuff can and absolutely will happen.

If you can find peace in "Relax. Nothing is under control," then bring that with you. Spend ten minutes before the interview quietly meditating on this. The best way to react to any interview snafus is to smile, take it easy, take a deep breath, and say, "No problem. Take your time."

Focus on being yourself, not being a person who needs to impress someone else. They're going to hire *you*, not some *version of you*. We all want to present our best selves, but sometimes presenting your best self is stressful. If I try to be anything other than myself, I come across as a bit of a wreck.

It can be tempting to think "you got this." There's only so much you can "got." Be prepared for something unexpected. Allow yourself to go with the flow. Don't let interruptions (even if they're on your side) stop you from being you. Hang on to that part of yourself that's present and in the moment.

Recruiter Jamie Contino has this suggestion:

> *The unexpected is bound to happen. How you respond will most likely affect your chances of getting the job. Luck favors the prepared, so take the time to research the company: look up your interviewers on LinkedIn and read press releases.*
>
> *If the interview goes off the rails, this may be a good indication as to how the company operates. If you're uncomfortable with the way the interview went, it happens and I promise you it's okay.*
>
> *Remember, you're interviewing them as much as they are interviewing you.*

Go be you. There's no one else who can do that.

Example

I mentioned in Misconception #13 that I found an article containing the 65 most important interview questions asked at nearly every interview.[19]

---

[19] https://www.theladders.com/career-advice/65-common-interview-questions-and-how-to-answer-them

I'll also be mentioning in Misconception #39 the concept of a fodder document, which is a database where I store all of the relevant points for my resume when I'm going to tailor it.

In preparation for recreational interviewing, I took some of the 65 questions and wrote several answers to them so I could pull from any of them in case I got asked.

Here are some of my verbatim notes:

What are your strengths? I know how to build high-performance teams. Every team that's worked with me was left in much better shape than when I joined.

I know how to take ambiguous problems, create order, and operationalize them.

I'm always bursting with ideas and I know how to back them up with understanding the work that goes into them.

I have a strong understanding of the business side of the organization. My peers are usually much stronger technicians, but weak on the business side. While I could be more technical, my career path is heading in a direction where I want to have a solid balance of both sides.

I know how to have crucial and difficult conversations because I know how to build very strong relationships. I've worked for years developing my communication skills to such an extent that I once had someone thank me for the way I fired them.

What are your weaknesses? I'm working to improve on putting too much on my plate. It's something I've done since I was a child and my dad would tell me that I bite off more than I can chew.

As an introvert, I have to manage how people perceive their interactions with me. I spend a lot of time listening, but that has sometimes come across as being inattentive or not caring.

I hope you can see I practice what I preach. And as Jeremy Wilson points out, when you speak to your failures, speak of them in a positive light to show how you might be working to strategically guard against that weakness.

Key Takeaways

1. Be prepared to be unprepared.
2. If something happens: stay calm, be chill.
3. Relax, nothing is under control.

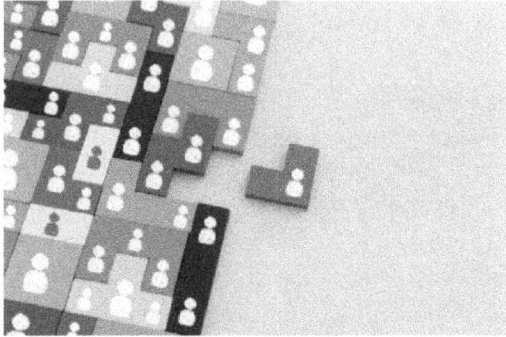

Misconception #40: Any Job is a Good Job

EVEN IF YOU haven't had a paycheck in a few months, let me assure you that some jobs are simply not good jobs. You might be totally desperate for meaningful work, for a paycheck, for health insurance, for a team to work with, for a sense of belonging. It's totally understandable. But, that doesn't mean *any* job is *a good* job.

Realistically, there are probably a hundred jobs you could get *right now*. If you're a business professional, you could go to the mall or to the local grocery store and probably find some position to fill. It may not pay you enough, it may not be fulfilling, it may not be the best move for your career, but a job is a job, right?

Well, think about what you'd be giving up.

If you get a job that's a bad job for you, you're allowing someone else to pay you for all that time you would have otherwise spent looking for a good job. They're essentially paying to take that time away from you—time you could have spent getting a better job. And it's not like this new job is going to be completely time-boxed or compartmentalized in your life. You're going to spend hours every week finding ways to cope with this new position, telling yourself, "It's not

199

that bad. At least I'm getting paid. At least I have health insurance."

But that stress adds up.

In a few weeks, you might be ready to explode from frustration. Now you're in a job you don't like, lying to everyone you meet that you're a long-term prospect at the company, building relationships you know you're just going to end as soon as you get the chance, and you're using all your free time to find another job. Now you have no time to go for a run, to decompress, to spend time with your family, to make dinner, to fulfill your spiritual obligations, and more.

It's easy to accept a job because you need a job. But a job is not just a job.

What to Do

It's super easy for me to say "keep going" when I'm employed and am not facing the stresses and problems you might be facing. But I can assure you that I've had close family members take the wrong jobs and it's wrecked them. When you're facing dire circumstances, it's really tempting to think, "Getting a job and a paycheck would really solve my problems." But it's even easier to ignore all the problems a bad job can cause in your life.

Like many things in life, you need to consider trade-offs. This is why it's so important to interview well and understand the costs.

If you have solid skills that were valuable pre-COVID, find a way to use those skills to make money for yourself, even if you're not working for a company. You might be able to get a short-term contract position. Or a part-time contract position. Or you can try freelance.

There are several ways to do what you do and make money. It doesn't have to be entirely in the hands of an employer. And if you do entrust your career to an employer for the short term, make sure it doesn't put your longer-term career goals at risk.

If you can make money on your own part time, you can still allow yourself the time to find a good job. If you end up with more work than you anticipated as a freelancer, you might be able to turn that into a full-time gig for yourself until something else comes along.

Here's sage advice from Jeremy Wilson:

> *The most precious thing in life is time. Is your job (or potential job) a good use of your time so you can accomplish your life dreams and provide your definition of happiness for you and your family? How does this job get you closer to your goals and happiness?*

It's okay if a job is just a stepping stone, just make sure to treat it as one.

Ellis has Something to Say

This is a hard one for Anthony because as he mentioned, he's in a very stable position in his life at the moment.

Real talk: sometimes you just gotta support yourself and your family, and any job truly is better than no job. Taking a job isn't the same as thinking that you're going to love the job, or that it's the end-all be-all. I was laid off in September 2020. The job market is tough.

I decided to do a freelance/entrepreneur pivot full-time in part because I hated corporate life but also because I was having a hard time finding something I could feel good about taking.

You have to do what you have to do to

support yourself and your family, and sometimes that means taking a shitty job. Anthony needs to remember what he said about the likelihood of you retiring in your position—it's unlikely. There's always another job after the one you have.

Anthony had written in some what-ifs above that I deleted because they just seemed...well, ridiculous. Some things like what if you're not good at the job and you get laid off? What if the company has a PR catastrophe; will that hinder your future prospects?

Those are what-ifs that you have to consider with EVERY JOB YOU TAKE.

If you have to take a job you don't feel great about because you NEED a job, and you're lucky enough to get an offer and your gut isn't telling you to run the other direction, TAKE IT.

As Anthony has mentioned, the best time to look for a job is when you don't need one.

Get your job, catch your breath, make the best of it, and keep looking. The last thing you need is Anthony's voice in your ear whispering what-ifs. This book will always be here to help you get that next position.

Key Takeaways

1. Consider the costs of getting a bad job you don't like or aren't good at.
2. Take the job if you need the job. Go for alternatives if it's a better option.
3. Use your skills to make money for yourself, even if it's just part-time.

Misconception #41: One Resume to Rule Them All!

YOU'VE HONED EVERY line break. You've crafted every verb. Your whole career is summarized in sets of bullets. You've squeezed it all into a couple of pages.

This is it. This is the moment. This is the one.

The one resume to rule them all.

When you turn this bad boy in for twenty different jobs today, it's gonna frikkin' blow the hiring managers' minds. Their faces are gonna melt off like it's the end of *Raiders of the Lost Ark*. Their hair's gonna blow back like that guy in the old Maxell audio cassette commercial. They're gonna read over this resume and say, "My God, it's full of stars."

While your resume may indeed be a work of perfection and high art, you also need to remember you might be casting your pearls before swine.

You are dealing with humans—humans who don't know you and who will spend *maybe* ten or twenty seconds looking over your resume.

Humans who might be looking at it on a tiny cell phone screen instead of the sRGB-calibrated 5K iMac screen on which it was *meant* to be viewed.

Humans who could be looking for a few keywords and a

standout sentence or two.

So, let's get back to reality: there is no perfect resume and you shouldn't use the same resume for every job opportunity.

There's no holy grail single message that will make every hiring manager bow at your feet and disrespect you with their filthy, unworthy job offers.

You have to meet them where they are.

This is why marketing teams spend so much time testing multiple messages for different markets to see what lands with a specific demographic. This is why companies have slogans that have nothing to do with their products getting plastered on billboards all over the world. This is why companies spend jillions of dollars hoping that their ad campaign is successful. Hone your message to reach *exactly* who you're hoping to reach so you can sell your product.

And the product you're selling right now is you.

What to Do

If you're selling you and your capabilities, then what is the message you're selling? Do you know your audience? Do you know your demographic? How are you marketing yourself? Is your resume in the same font (Times New Roman) as every other one they're getting? Do you have a slogan that sells your ability to fill the role? What is it that sets you apart when a hiring manager or recruiter is looking at your resume in the midst of hundreds of others?

Here's how I handled my resume.

I have two documents: the resume and all the fodder. My fodder document has dozens of bullet points written for every job I've had. There's no way I can summarize my seven years at one company in four different roles with just a few bullets. Plus, there's no way I can remember everything I did in those roles if I keep it to just a few bullets. The fodder document helps me remember everything I did in a role and gives me options for tailoring my resume for a job.

When I study a job description, I paste the whole thing into a notes file. I strike through everything that's filler or irrelevant. I underline all the key statements. I color the text of related points so I can see what the general themes are for the job. I'll even paste the job description into a word cloud just to see which words get repeated and see what stands out.

In other words, I do a lot of research before I even think about applying for a position. It's worth mentioning that I applied for probably 12-15 positions in 2020 and had 3 interviews. Remember, it's more luck of the draw than it is skill. But each hiring manager that interviewed me told me how impressed they were with my resume and how it seemed like I was a great fit for the position.

This was no accident—I spent a lot of time crafting my message so it met them where they were.

Recruiter Jamie Contino shares resume perspective:

> *Many companies take the time to write great job descriptions because they are really looking for the right candidate. They cater their JD for a reason and you should do the same to your resume. Look at the JD and pull out key words and responsibilities, look at the required skill set section AND the preferred skills. Expand on these topics; remember your resume does not have to fit onto one page, especially if you have seven to ten years of experience. Do parse down the noise on your resume if it doesn't pertain to the job you are applying to. I cannot stress this enough, there is no one resume to rule them all. If you put the work in to get noticed, it will pay off.*

There is no perfect resume. It's not art. It's a marketing campaign to get someone to invest—to buy my time and keep me from going into business on my own.

Key Takeaways

1. There's no perfect resume.
2. What's perfect to you may not be perfect for getting a job.
3. Find ways to market yourself to a hiring manager or recruiter, just like companies do to their customers.
4. Consider using a fodder document so you can easily tailor your resume.

Misconception #42: It's Okay to talk about 2020 and 2021

2020 WAS A tough year for so many. Hundreds of thousands of families dealt with death and long-term illness just from COVID-19. That's in addition to all the deaths we normally have to deal with.

And those of us who didn't die or lose someone also had to face:

- The effects of a global pandemic (lockdowns, stay at home orders, remote work).
- Economic collapse and record job losses.
- Police brutality.
- The worst presidential election season ever.
- Racial tensions.
- Record wildfires across the U.S.
- Cancellation of nearly every recreational event.
- School closures and kids at home ALL. THE. TIME.
- No travel/vacations.
- Increases in depression and other mental health problems.

It's difficult to paint 2020 in a positive light.

When I was asked to speak at a webinar earlier in 2020, someone asked me whether it's okay to talk about the difficulties of 2020 at a job interview.[20]

This is a risky situation.

If you're in a sales situation, do you really want to bring up a negative topic or experience, especially with a person you don't know? You might have a strong stance on one aspect of 2020 (like a presidential candidate) and the interviewer may have the opposite. Or you might be an observer of one of these difficult 2020 situations while the interviewer may have been a participant or a victim.

There's too much opportunity for something to go wrong and steer the message away from "I'm a great candidate for your job" to "2020 was a crappy year and this interview is a tough conversation."

It's not necessarily right to completely avoid talking about the difficulties you faced during or after the pandemic, but I wouldn't spend much time on it as a topic because even if you try to make light of it, it could just spin out of control.

What to Do

The point of a job interview is to move forward on the path toward getting hired—it is not about commiserating or talking about the weather or politics or anything like that.

If you can find a way to align a piece of information with your pitch as the best candidate for the job, then use it. Otherwise, I recommend avoiding the elephant in the room that that could trigger another person's emotions about the craziness of the past few years.

During the early 2020 webinar, the discussion went

[20] https://www.youtube.com/watch?v=EYjRuQ3_GlM

towards, "What if I lost my job this year because of COVID? Should I mention that? What if I really need a paycheck?"

The problem with this approach is that it makes the hiring about *you* and not about *solving the hiring manager's problem.* You are interviewing to fill a role that an employer is offering. You are not interviewing so you can get hired. That may be your intention, but you have no leverage in the situation.

Whether it was 2019 or 2025, I'd be giving the same advice. If it has the chance of putting a negative shadow on the hiring manager's perception of their interaction with you, it's likely not going to get you the job. It's the hellscape of corporate reality. "Don't talk about real life. Talk about how you're here to make my company money."

I wish it was different, but it isn't.

As mentioned in the preface of this book, the COVID-19 pandemic was a 24-month-long kidney punch.

Who knows what the decade will bring?

Regardless, don't let it win.

Ellis has Something to Say

As usual, I agree with Anthony to a point. If you have an interviewer ask you about a gap in your resume or a job not in line with your career path, I think it is acceptable, even appropriate, to say, "In 2020, my company suffered from the economic downturn and I was part of layoffs."

Then take the opportunity to pivot hard into your value, not into 2020. "With my time off, I taught myself a new coding language and these relevant skills in order to keep myself abreast of recent industry innovations."

Key Takeaways

1. First rule of Job Club: don't talk about anything that'll cast a bad light on the conversation.
2. Try to keep your interview positive. Don't focus on the negativity of the year.
3. Don't make assumptions about the interviewer(s) perspective on current events, especially about political topics.
4. Be awesome and be yourself.

Misconception #43: You Don't Like Your Job

ONE DAY YOU love your job. Three years later, you hate it. What's that about? May I suggest it's not entirely the job itself?

In working with a coach, I've had to learn about myself and my values. Six years ago, I couldn't articulate my values. One session with my values coach, Jenn Kaye, and I was in tears in my office at work as she basically tore into my life with barely any prior relationship.[21] She cut right to my heart. It was amazing.

Why? What got me so emotional? What's the big deal?

Learning about my values gave me the secrets to understanding my motivations. My values were the keys to saying Yes or No to an opportunity. Suddenly, I had the greatest possible filter for next steps in my life. If I faced a difficult decision, I could simply ask myself, "Is this in alignment with my values? Am I going to be aligned with this in six to twelve months or am I just getting excited about an idea right now?"

Jenn taught me so much about myself through my values and pointed me to some great resources, including the

---

[21] http://jennkaye.com/

211

Consulting Resource Group at crgleader.com. It was there that I learned "motivation is only required for things that don't interest me."

That was huge.

Another big lesson in learning my values is that a frustrated life is out of alignment with its values. I learned that my frustration with myself and my career was largely about being out of alignment with my values and not just "I don't like my job anymore."

That's when the light went on in my head. I started testing this hypothesis of value alignment with all of my employees and my peers. Sure enough, it looked to be true. I was even able to help people begin enjoying their jobs again. It felt like a magic trick, but it wasn't. It was just a developed ability to help people reframe their daily experience through their values.

It was then that I learned that people don't like or dislike their jobs. Rather, they like or dislike how their day-to-day decisions and actions are perpetuating a life they want to live.

What to Do

Find a values coach. Call them. Pay them (if you can). Have a session with them. Change your life.

It's that simple.

If you can't afford to pay a coach, then go on YouTube and check out free values-based content. (For example, you can go to JennKaye.com and study my value coach's content.) There's a ton of great, free content from CRG Leader as well. Dr. Keis and other values-based coaches have written excellent, affordable books as well. The online VPI assessment from CRG Leader is affordable. There's plenty of free and low-cost educational material that will help identify your values.

When you know your values, you know how you are

intrinsically motivated. You will how your life is in or out of alignment. You might find you value security and stability, but your home life is kinda outta whack. Instead of attributing your professional frustration to personal frustration, you might just think it's all about your job situation.

Emotionally, we're like a big, goopy pile of spaghetti and syrup. There's no pulling the professional noodles apart from the personal noodles. And even if we do, there's a sticky, syrupy mess everywhere. Which leaves us with a question: who put syrup on spaghetti in the first place? I mean, that's not even a *thing* unless you're an elf from the North Pole searching for his father.

A values coach can provide clarity in unexpected ways. My coach, Jenn, used something called the Values Preference Indicator (VPI) from CRG Leader.[22] The guy who runs that site, Dr. Ken Keis, provides great content on the site and in the values assessment report. For example, he says that when your values are unfulfilled you start to feel fear and anxiety. Why? Because the opposites of our values are our fears. *mic drop*

Think about that for a second. If you value honesty, you have a fear of people lying to you. If you value creativity, you fear losing creative control of your work. If you value independence, you fear being micromanaged or unable to operate with autonomy. If you value security, you fear instability.

Crazy, right? Crazy like a fox.

The point is this: learning your values can open your eyes about your behaviors and your emotions. When you're living in high alignment with your values, then all is well. Low anxiety, high satisfaction. When you're out of alignment with your values (even in just one part of your life), anxiety goes up

---

[22] https://crgleader.com/product/values-preference-indicator/

and satisfaction goes down.

Is it the case that you dislike your job or are you living out of alignment with your values? That's where a coach can help you. The coach has externality you lack. Coaches exist for this very reason. They show what you need to do and how to do it. They have critical experience and insight that's hard to come up with on your own.

I've talked a lot of good people out of quitting their jobs. Why? Because I was able to show them that they won't be happy in their next role. They're filling that value-alignment-shaped hole with the novelty of a new workplace, a new role, a different salary, new relationships and more. It's just a distraction.

Just because you're unhappy with your job doesn't mean you need to quit. It doesn't even mean you're unhappy with your job. There might be something else going on. And that's okay. We're all stressed and trying to figure things out.

But if you've got a job, don't feel like you need to quit. And if you're frustrated about anything else in life, just remember that it might spill over into your work.

Ellis has Something to Say

There is a good chance that this is not the perfect time in your life to start paying a coach, especially if you are unemployed against your will. This is the problem with coaches—they're accessible to those with the money to employ them.

If you've been laid off, did your employer provide access to an outplacement firm? I've never had fantastic experiences with them, but use them anyway. Take all the free help you can get. Same with any access to online learning— take what you can get.

If you're a college graduate, check in with the alumni association at your school. Do they offer free or discounted services to their alums? What about your city, county, or local library— do they offer free career resources you can harness? For example, Maricopa County where I live offers ARIZONA@WORK career services to those over 18 who can legally work in the U.S.[23] *Or you can try something like Mentor Works*[24] *(disclaimer: I have not worked with and this is not an endorsement, just the fruits of some online research).*

When needs must, get creative. There are many free resources we never know about until we dig.

Also let the record reflect that Anthony only added his resources above after I said something about it to him and wrote my own section. Yes, I claim credit.

Y U SO PETTY ELLIS?!

Key Takeaways

1. Learn your values, live them out, and get rid of whatever keeps you out of alignment with them. If you can, find a values coach. If not, take the CRG Leader VPI.
2. Consider ways you might be unhappy because of values, not because of your job circumstances.

---

[23] https://www.maricopa.gov/5226/Find-A-Job-Through-Our-Career-Services
[24] https://mentorworks.com/

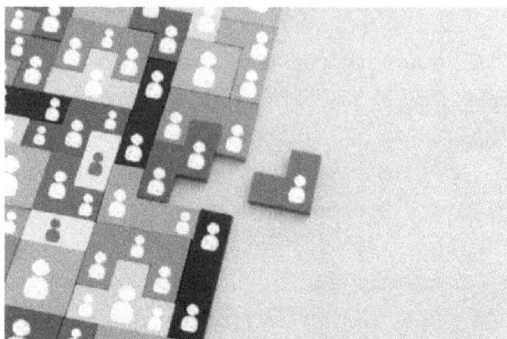

Misconception #44: You Know What You Want in your Next Job

HAVE YOU EVER watched a movie or a TV show and thought, "Oh, I totally know what's happening next?"

What's that about? Why does that happen?

The writers have set everything up so the next move in the story makes sense. As an astute viewer, you're going through this very experience. You predict what happens next in the show because it's where the writers want the plot to go. [That or their writing is very formulaic.]

It's kind of like what I'm doing right now. Can you see where I'm going? Am I setting it up for you? Can you knock it out of the park?

When looking at your career, your previous jobs and your life circumstances, it can be easy to jump to conclusions, saying, "I know where this is going." It's because you have a story arc and, frankly, no one has thought about your life more than you.

You're likely to pick a next step that makes the most sense according to the story you've crafted in your head.

And that's totally cool. Ain't nothin' wrong with that.

BUT...

You're probably making assumptions about what's next

and crafting imaginary blinders that shape your next steps. This is a difficult thing to avoid. You want a next step that makes sense, that's not out in left field, but it's unlikely a crazy opportunity will fall in your lap. (Hey, I didn't say it's impossible. It's just unlikely, all right?)

When you think about the next step in your career, are you actually thinking about what you want, or are you thinking about what makes the most sense for the story you're writing in your head?

I'll leave you with a Jordan Peterson quote I don't fully understand:

> *Betray your destiny and see how long it takes you to be drowning in a storm. What's calling you to be your best is exactly the thing that's pushing you forward to manifest yourself most fully in the world.*

I think he's saying something about challenging yourself, but who knows with that guy?

What to Do

There's nothing wrong with writing your own story. Why would there be? The key thing to understand is you may be building unnecessary constraints into your job search. This may cause you to opt out of opportunities that *could* be pretty awesome.

For example, I spent the first 16 years of my career working in the education technology space. First I worked at a K-12 school for several years. Then I worked at Arizona State University. Then I worked at Pearson Education, my first corporate gig—still in education. The next job very easily could have been in education, but thankfully I had grown tired of the slow pace and the spending-hours-to-do-minutes-of-work frustration.

But it took 16 years to realize that I wanted something less safe and less government-y/tax-funded. I rebelled against my own career and left the 36,000-person international corporation. Then I found myself in a small, boutique software development agency with about 70 people. Talk about a change. What a breath of fresh air.

Would I have found the job if I hadn't spent 16 years in the same industry? Maybe not. I wanted a narrative violation. I wanted something out of left field. And I got it. But it was largely a reactionary move away from the education industry.

As I've mentioned ad nauseum, I've looked at *a lot of resumes*. Many of them follow a story arc, like a movie or TV show. We like familiarity, and hiring managers like continuity. It feels good to say, "Yes, I know the industry. I've been working in it for eight years." We feel like experts and that's a good feeling. But that feeling is a legit trade-off.

I've beaten this horse to death. Developing expertise can pigeonhole you. You can become a niche expert which has risks. It's important to be aware of these trade-offs.

Realize that knowing what you want in your next job might mean you're looking for something that's comfortable. Comfort can lead to stagnation, or it can lead to deep expertise. Know yourself and know what will pay off in the long run.

If you think you can't do what I did, check out this LinkedIn message I got just a few days ago from a former coworker:

> *Your posts really helped me in making the decision to move to my current company. I know that may sound strange, but I have tended to play it safe in recent years working for companies that were established and it was a big deal for me to*

consider a startup. I am excited for the challenge and being in an environment where I can truly grow and create!

Key Takeaways

1. Consider how your career may have been led or motivated by safety.
2. If you've been in one industry for a decade or more, consider whether you may be pigeonholing yourself in a job that might not exist in another decade.
3. Find ways your skills may easily transfer into another industry. Try it out. Ask your network.

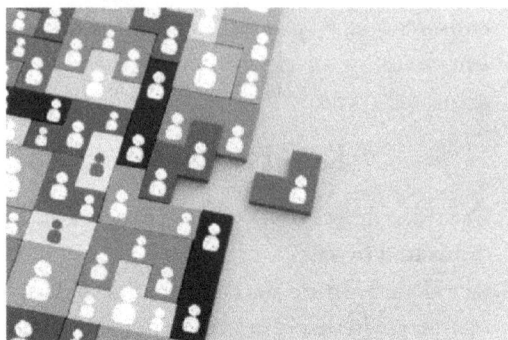

Misconception #45: There's Nothing you Can do to Stand Out

ONE DAY MANY years ago, we had a woman come into the office to sing her job application to HR. Like, literally sing a song in person and out loud as her job application.

She was not a professional singer, nor was she a good one. It was a moment of stunning bravery. Mid-song, her body and voice were shaking. It took everything she had to keep it under control. In front of the entire project management team (where the HR office was located), she sang:

> I've always been a fighter.
> When bad times come around,
> I'm not gonna take it anymore.
> I'm not going to let it get me down,
> I'm gonna get back up and stand my ground.
> I'm gonna show who's boss
> to everyone who's watching.
> Fighting evil all around,
> I'm gonna run those bad guys out of town.
> Cuz I'm a superhero,
> I'll keep on flying.

Was it super cringe? Absolutely. Was it crazy admirable? Heck yeah. The look on our HR director's face was priceless. He just stared in bewilderment for two and a half minutes.

Yes, I have it on video. No, I won't send you the link.

Nevertheless, this lady had chutzpah and I'll never forget her. Did she get the job? No, unfortunately she didn't. But did she leave a permanent impression? Yep.

Then there was a friend who received a pizza at work with a job application and resume taped inside the box. Was it bribery? Maybe. Did it get the candidate an interview? Yes.

Or there was that time someone applied for a job with my peer's department and the resume was a one-liner: "I'm a genius and you won't regret hiring me."

Did we talk to him? Yes.

Did we hire him? No, but he got an interview.

I shared in an earlier misconception how I applied for a job I knew I wasn't qualified for. The reason I got the call: I was told I "knew how to write a sentence." Even being a good writer can make you stand out.

There are still plenty of ways to stand out and get an interview. It's so easy to apply for jobs nowadays (just one theoretical click on LinkedIn) that doing *something* beyond applying can make you really stand out from the crowd.

As we've already said, luck favors the prepared. If you get the interview by doing something outrageous, be prepared to ace the interview. Don't compromise your integrity. Your ploy doesn't have to be racy, outlandish, or awkward.

You can be yourself and go above and beyond if you're really after a particular role at a particular company (and you know that move is going to get you in instead of get you ruled out).

What to Do

When you want to really get the attention of a hiring manager, find out a little about the company culture and acceptable behaviors tolerated by employees. I'm sure Ellis will have commentary about how it's easier for me being a dude and sending a pizza because I'm a tech bro (which are valid comments), but there are ways to get attention without being inappropriate.

It can be strategically responding to tweets or LinkedIn posts. It can be contributing to an open source project the company's working on. It can be meeting someone who's on the same team. It can be a book in the mail. It can be many, many things.

Just don't cross lines. Don't be inappropriate, don't do anything unethical, don't bribe and don't do anything that can be misconstrued. An email to the hiring manager saying, "I just wanted to make a personal connection since you probably see hundreds of people applying for this role," can be enough. Or find a mutual connection to make an introduction.

There are a lot of ways to stand out.

If you don't want to go beyond the job application itself, you can always do something like having your resume specifically graphically designed for that role/company. You can print it out on high quality paper and leave a handwritten thank you note. You can do a creative project or donate your time to a cause the company/hiring manager cares about.

To stand out, some people put funny messages in their job application. For example, we used to ask every job candidate to answer the question "What makes you unique?" Most of the answers were super-duper bland, but occasionally we'd get something great and that was enough to make me say, "Okay, they tried and I'll reward them with a phone call."

There's an article on HuffPost with a few examples of

standing out:

- Listing "gator hunting" as a skill.
- Setting up the resume to be sung to the tune of The Brady Bunch theme song.
- Decorating the resume with pink rabbits.
- Recognition as "Homecoming Prom Prince in 1984."

Look, they can't all be winners, but if you want to stand out, figure something out that represents you and is in alignment with what the company wants to see.

No one wants to hire a boring fart—except for actuaries who are, quite literally, boring farts.

Ellis has Something to Say

Anthony has me pegged. Before I talk about how it seems way easier to get attention in unconventional ways if you're a dude, can I just say I am not surprised that the chanteuse did not get the job? Please do not sing your resume unsolicited. While I applaud this woman's gumption, I also caution against looking desperate.

I agree with Anthony that sometimes you have to be unconventional in getting attention. If you're a woman and your target is a man, sending a pizza could work in your favor if they don't know what you look like (hard with LinkedIn).

Why do I think this? Because no matter what you look like if you're a woman, meanings get misconstrued and intentions misinterpreted. It's really not a huge step for a lot of people from "She sent me a pizza" to "She'll do anything to get this job." Wink-wink.

I'm absolutely NOT saying that if you send a male hiring manager a pizza and he sexually harasses you, that it's in any way your fault. For me, I am cautious about this because I do not want to open myself up to more of this behavior (while I haven't had nearly as much of it as many others, I've had plenty enough of it in my life). As we know, women often suffer the consequences of these actions. (And if you don't know, please take time to research sexual harassment retaliation.)

It's also harder to decorate your resume in pink rabbits if you're a woman, because then you'll be fighting the same stereotypes as Elle Woods in Legally Blonde. And yes, she prevailed mightily, but she is fictional. When men decorate their resume in pink bunnies, it's funny and attention grabbing. When women do, it's "immature" or "pathetic" or generally looked down on because dudes don't want that kind of vibe. And God forbid you put you were homecoming queen on your resume! Oh Anthony, so well-intentioned.

If you're trying something new to stand out, only do what rings true and safe. That might be pink bunnies on your resume. That's cool. I don't know everything, and I don't know you. I'd be happy to hear that it got you a job and publicly proclaim myself wrong on Twitter.

I've never tried a gimmick, but if I did, I would do something in line with the company personality or values. I worked for one company that was really proud of its cereal bar—free cereal all day every day (it's what passes for a perk in the Phoenix area), and they wrote about it on their website. If I wanted to go the imagery route, I might have sprinkled my resume with virtual cereal or sent a bowl and spoon to the hiring manager.

Key Takeaways

1. Don't sing your job application.
2. Find unconventional ways to stand out that are professional and fit with the culture of the company or the personality of the hiring manager.
3. Consider putting an "Easter egg" in your resume or cover letter to see who notices it. (Remember: keep it professional.)

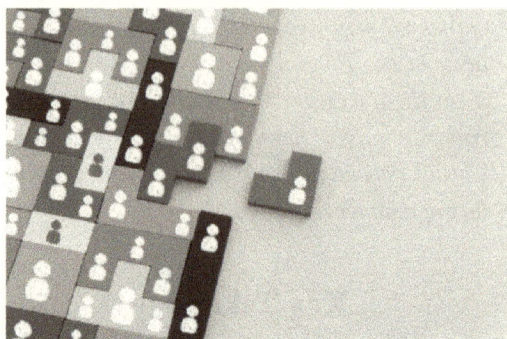

Misconception #46: Talking to a Recruiter is "an Offer"

I CAN'T TELL you how many times I've heard people say, "I've gotten offers for 25% more than I'm making now working fewer hours with better benefits." My advice almost every time is, "You should totally take that job! Take it right now! Don't be a fool!"

Then they respond with, "Well, I mean, it was a call from a recruiter." Or, "That's what the LinkedIn message says. I'll have to follow up."

Of course, they can't take the offer because the offer isn't an offer at all. It's empty—bait from recruiters who know they can pull a fast one.

I'm smart enough to know when I'm being tested. And I'm smart enough to call people out on their BS. I've worked with enough recruiters to know the good ones and the ones who can't be trusted.

Most of the time, it's young, inexperienced people giving me these lines. They're in the tech industry with sharks in the recruiting waters who want to place anyone they can at a high salary in a cushy tech job. They send out LinkedIn messages that say, "I've got the perfect job for you at this incredible salary. You can work four days a week, get free health and dental, huge signing bonuses, and the company is on the rise."

Sounds too good to be true because it is.

When you talk to a recruiter, you don't have an offer; you have an idea. At *best*, it's an opportunity. But not all opportunities are won.

Good recruiters don't entice you from the get-go. They want to get to know you. They want to make sure you're not going to be a candidate that tarnishes their good reputation. I've helped many good recruiters find good candidates. They operate on trust. They don't take bad candidates. They don't send LinkedIn messages promising the huge leaps in salary and benefits.

They usually start with, "Let's get to know each other. I have an opportunity you might fit." They're cautious. Their skepticism comes from a need to maintain a strong relationship with their client. They want to place good people in good jobs and keep their working relationship going with the hiring company.

What to Do

If you get a crazy offer in a LinkedIn message and the recruiter shows no interest in getting to know you, that's a red flag. It's the grown-up equivalent of the guy in the unmarked, white van saying, "Hey kid, do you like free candy?"

Just like we're hard-wired to seek out fats and sugars, we also love a good job offer. (I know, that's a stretch of a metaphor, but roll with it.) There's something so heartwarming about knowing someone sees more value in you than your last job did. "They were paying you $20/hr? I think you're worth at least $23/hr." It feels good. They like me. They *really like me!*

But talk is cheap. These kinds of "offers" are meant to start a conversation and reel you in. If you were making $55K and the recruiter tells you they can get you $65K, you'll want

227

to talk to them. And if they can get you an offer at $60K, that's good for you and good for them. Some lower-end recruiters might even promise you $65K knowing that a company's budget is only $60K. They'll bust their butt to get you cash money.

They'll do everything they can to persuade you to take that offer, because they get somewhere between 15 to 30% of your base salary as a placement fee. They're incentivized to get you the highest salary possible.

Along the way, you might feel a little icky. That's okay. It's how we learn.

A solid, reputable recruiter (like the ones featured in this book) will instead reach out to you, get to know you, understand what drives you (like your values), and think of positions for which you'd be a good fit. For example, Allen Plunkett has a 90-page training document on how to find good candidates. He specifically instructs his team to look for A-level candidates because he only recruits for A-level jobs and his company's reputation is the most important thing about his business.

Allen knows there are a zillion recruiters out there, but there aren't a zillion reputable recruiters who know the cost of a tarnished relationship. He instructs his team to listen, ask questions, listen some more, take notes, keep listening, and have meaningful conversations. He doesn't want to place a bad candidate in a good job, nor does he want to place a good candidate in a bad job.

Recruiters like Allen will never reach out with a fake offer, an inflated, teaser salary number or some other form of bribe. They know what the market pays, they know the good companies, and they know where to find quality candidates. They'll invest in you, even if it takes two to three months to find you a position, because they want to build a good relationship with you for your next job search while maintaining a good relationship with the client (the employer).

So, when you get one of those emails or LinkedIn messages promising you the world, don't fall for it. You can do what I do and say, "Not interested." Or you can ignore the message altogether. I've faced no discernible cost with either response. The crummy recruiters will just move on and look a viable candidate who will respond.

Key Takeaways

1. Getting hypothetical numbers from a recruiter is not getting an offer. It's a hypothetical discussion about a theoretical future.
2. Less-than-stellar recruiters will entice you on LinkedIn with fantasy numbers. They know what you're making now and they know what would sound good.
3. Finding a good recruiter will get you much further over the course of your career than working with a one-off.

Misconception #47: You Should Only Apply Once

IF YOU'VE NEVER hired anyone before, you've probably never used something called an Applicant Tracking System, or ATS. Put simply, an ATS is one of the worst pieces of software ever designed. Its only redeeming feature is its exorbitant cost.

In all seriousness, ATS software is very complex because it needs to do so much. It's targeted at HR professionals (who never seem to complain loud enough to get great software). In my experience with ATSs, new job applications pile up. The newest applicants are at the top of the list, but you can typically sort by a few different columns.

The ATSs I've used didn't filter out applicants who applied more than once. Maybe they do that now, but that's probably not a feature most small and medium sized businesses use. In my experience, it never hurts to put your name at the top of the list by applying more than once.

Like email, you don't want to spam the system and be annoying. Nor do you want to be cutesy and try to get around the system by applying under multiple similar names. Think of it like an email, but you have no idea who the recipient is or whether they're going to open your application. The probability of getting dozens of applications per day is pretty high.

I don't know about you, but when I get dozens of emails a day, I start becoming desensitized to incoming mail. Several hiring managers I know feel the same way. Checking the ATS every day can feel like checking yet another email inbox, but requires more work.

There might only be time to check the latest five or 10 applicants. Or there might be an internal recruiter who's helping to fill the role, but doesn't have the same critical eye for applicant review as I might as the hiring manager.

The point is, there's (probably) no system that shows your name and the number of times you've applied. I've never seen an ATS penalize a person for applying more than once. However, if the hiring manager or recruiter sees your name too many times, then you might look desperate.

What to Do

I don't have a hard recommendation on this one, but like I said, it can't hurt to apply more than once.

If the job is still open two or three weeks after you first applied, that's probably a good time to apply again. If the job remains open for another two to three weeks, I might consider applying again. If I still don't hear anything, then I'd either assume they're not interested or I'd find a way to reach the hiring manager.

I've seen people use variations on their own name, like including their middle initial or a misspelling of their name. That's fine by me, but it might bother some hiring managers. The thing is, what are you going to do when you get the hiring manager's attention?

Here's what is important: if the recruiter calls you after you've applied three times, are you going to win them over?

Remember, we could all be more like Jeremy Wilson.

Prove you're worth their time and attention.

Prove you're worth more than the salary they're offering.
Be the person they absolutely needed to talk to.

Carmen West's experience with ATSs is a bit different
from mine. I've not used the giant, corporate, expensive
ATSs, but she has.

Here's what she has to say:

> *From an ATS perspective, you can apply as many
> times as you like, but it doesn't move you up in
> the queue.*
>
> *What moves you up in terms of showing up
> on the dashboard is the level of experience and
> expertise. That system is programmed for hits
> [matches on the keywords]. That's the reality. It's
> programmed for hits. The more hits you get, the
> more times that you will show up for that
> particular role you applied for. Then you'll show
> up on the dashboard so they make the first call.*
>
> *That's all you're trying to do, get those hits
> and get that phone screen.*

I like to think of it this way: Applying for a job is my way of
getting someone's attention.

Once I have their attention, then the rest should be easy.
Getting the attention is the hard part because the hiring
manager's attention is in high demand. But once we exchange
emails, shake hands, whatever, it should be smooth sailing.

The application process gives them a reason to call me,
not a reason to hire me.

Speaking to me and learning about what I can do for them
is the reason to hire me.

Key Takeaways

1. Most companies use an Applicant Tracking System. There's a high probability it's doing more than it should and affecting the visibility of your application.
2. ATSs can be gamed and you can try some different techniques to do so. But they are getting smarter, so your mileage may vary.
3. Applying for a role is like a sales gig. Once you get a qualified lead, it's your job to convert them.

Misconception #48: The Grass is Greener on the Other Side

THROUGHOUT MOST OF this guide, we've assumed you don't have a job. But, as I write this sentence in June 2021, the U.S. Bureau of Labor Statistics has reported hours ago that there were 9.3 *million* jobs available on the last day of April 2021. The economy has been continuously growing as U.S. vaccination rates increase and people return to normal life.

We can safely assume there are at least 10 million jobs available right now. Where I live in Arizona, our governor recently promised $2,000 to eligible workers who get a new job ("Arizona Back to Work"). These are basically government-funded signing bonuses to get a job. Incredible.

But, we have a problem.

Despite the free money and the *millions* of available jobs with full- and part-time remote work, people still aren't leaping off the couch to get a job. What gives?

I know people who tell me they make more money on unemployment than if they were working. They like that lifestyle. Good for them, I guess? I'm sure the unemployment benefits will run out and getting a job will pay more, but for now, some people choose not to work.

I also know other employed people who thought about

getting another job, but realized they actually like what they do. When they think about the idea of getting another job, going through the whole process, getting interviewed, negotiating—ugh, it's just tiresome.

As the old saying goes: You don't know what you have 'til you lose it.

Whether you're home and happily unemployed or you're stuck in a job that meets your needs, it doesn't mean you need to jump into something different. But something led you this far into a guide on getting a new job.

What's up with *that?*

What to Do

My former boss, who we shall call Steve because that is his actual name, told me he's been in a pretty boring job for the past seven or nine years. (LinkedIn says it's seven years and ten months.) We were drinking a bit of beer at the time when we were talking about this, so some details may be fuzzy.

Anyway, Steve told me that he read my book *Clueless at The Work* and thought about getting another job. He loved the idea of recreational interviewing. He set up the automated job alerts with relevant search terms. He got the weekly and daily digests. And then he realized something...

As boring as his job is, he actually likes where he works. He's acquired skills he wouldn't have otherwise picked up. He even ended up getting a retention bonus in company stock for sticking around through the pandemic. Given his background in academia and education technology, he realized he'd never actually been given a meaningful retention bonus before.

The more he read about other jobs, the more he thought, "Oh, I wouldn't like that company." Or, "Several aspects of that job sound pretty unpleasant." He kept looking for greener pastures, but he couldn't find them.

When I met Steve nearly 20 years ago, he had a bigger

role in his department. The work was much more interesting and creative, but the pay was miserable and there was no future. Where he is now, there actually is a future. He's learning Adobe Illustrator. Sure, he's pretty much only working with esoteric charts and graphs now, but he's developed a unique skill.

It wasn't until he started looking for another job that he realized what he had.

There's power in wanting what you have.

Ellis has Something to Say

I just want to state for the record that I take issue with Anthony's portrayal of people on unemployment as not wanting to get off the couch.

Unemployment saved my family when both my husband and I were laid off in 2020. We weren't about to go hungry, but it meant we didn't have to run through all of our savings. My husband used up all of his unemployment benefits and deliberately waited to get a gig/low-paying job until his benefits ran out. Why? Because 1. Gig jobs pay absolute shit 2. I was scaling up my new business with Anthony and my husband took over the house and childcare, which he could not do if he was working. 3. Low-paying jobs paid less than unemployment.

To this I say, it's a problem with the market, not the job seeker. Use this guide to get the best job you can and give a firm middle finger to governors who will pay you to get a shitty job but not do anything to make sure people can actually live off the wages from said job.

And hey, if you're lucky like Steve and

realize your work is boring, but has a lot going for it, that's fantastic. You don't have to apply elsewhere. But if you ever do, you know where to come for excellent advice and hot political takes.

Key Takeaways

1. If you're reading this book and you're this far in, there's a good chance you want to get off the couch.
2. Ain't nothing wrong with realizing you're bored.
3. Maybe you're not as bored as you think you are.

Misconception #49: Sharing your Salary is Fine

IN *CLUELESS AT THE WORK*, I shared the story of how I applied for a senior-level technology role and signed an offer letter that didn't have the word "Senior" in the title. The senior aspects included a higher bonus tier, better benefits, and more. I didn't think much of it until bonus payout time came about. I emailed my boss and he said, "Oh the job title was señor, not senior. :)"

Yes, that's literally what the email said.

He thought it was funny. I wanted to punch a hole in a wall. My dumb mistake cost me money and probably a few years in climbing the corporate ladder. When I came to this realization, I spoke with a peer who told me, "Yeah, you made a big mistake. But let me save you from making another mistake: never share your salary with anyone who doesn't need to know it."

I asked why.

He said, "Sharing your salary does one of two things: Makes the other person feel good about what they're making, or makes them upset about not making as much as you do."

And sure enough, I was promoted to a managerial role a couple years later only to find that all my former peers were making quite a bit more money than I was. And some of them were *definitely* not earning their full salary as much as others.

There was one person on the team who never did the job well enough to get promoted and never did poorly enough to get fired. That person was making about $17,000 more per year than I was, and I was this person's manager. I was infuriated.

How could this be? How could life be so unfair?

Later on in my career, I was looking for another job and the recruiters kept asking, "What are you making in your current role?" I told them the truth, because mommy always told me to tell the truth.

Turns out that mom's advice wasn't so great.

The more experience I got, the more I realized that sharing my salary wasn't the right approach. It gave other people leverage over me. For advise, I went back to my friend who told me not to share my salary. He said his standard response is: "I always say I am happy to earn the salary commensurate with the position."

Not a bad idea.

Ellis has Something to Say

Oh boy, does Ellis have something to say.

First, let's separate this into two instances: Sharing your salary with your coworkers, and sharing your salary in a negotiation setting.

I agree with Anthony: Do not share your salary in a negotiation setting. I too have made this mistake. Don't do it.

Now let's get to the part where I disagree with Anthony, because that's the fun part. I might not go as far as saying that keeping salaries secret is a tool of the patriarchy, maybe.

Anthony is right, it is a real pisser to realize

your peers, or even your subordinates, are making more than you. You know who experiences this all the time? Women. BIPOC. Some say those groups are at fault for not negotiating enough, or not sticking up for themselves enough, and I will chastise those people for turning this into their/our fault (I am a woman, not BIPOC). I will also tell you that women and BIPOC are generally told to be grateful for what they can get and in fact are often maligned by men and women alike for being aggressive. BIPOC are perceived as being worth less, or more grateful to even have a job. But let's bring this back to the workplace context.

If women don't know they're making less than men (which they are—yes, really,[25] and BIPOC too[26]), how are they supposed to know how much they are worth? Why are women/BIPOC still low-balled? Why are people still low-balled? Why is negotiation even a thing? Oh right, because in business it's not about objective measures of worth; it's about getting as much work out of you as possible for the lowest possible salary, even if you're a vanity hire like Prince Harry at BetterUp.

When we hide pay scales and forbid employees from talking about them, it creates a culture of fear and perpetuates disparity. It's entirely unfair that Anthony made $17,000 less than someone lazier and less-qualified. Why does keeping it a secret make it better? Are Anthony's

---

[25] https://www.payscale.com/data/gender-pay-gap
[26] https://www.payscale.com/data/racial-wage-gap

feelings worth $17,000?

I get this isn't necessarily something you can change unless you're someone like Jeremy Wilson, who's in an executive position who can make policies around pay and transparency. But if you, like me, would like to end the stigma about knowing what people are paid so you can be paid fairly, I welcome you to join my rant.

Final thought: why are Americans so weird about money? Why is understanding how your compensation compares to others a thief of joy? And why is it that when we find out we are staggeringly undervalued, as Anthony did, we can't do anything about it?

What to Do

There are a lot of approaches to salary negotiation and sharing salary. In fact, entire books have been written about this very subject. I'm not going to do justice to the entire genre of salary negotiation, but I can offer the following tips:

1. If you're working with an external recruiter, let them help you figure out the right salary. If they ask what you're currently making, you might start by qualitatively comparing what you make to the market value for that role. You can say, "I believe I'm making under market value and I'd like to make above market value." Some recruiters might say, "Okay, what do you believe is your market value?" That's a very different conversation than "How much are you making in your current role?"

2. Companies always have a salary range in mind when they're hiring. On the lower end of the salary range, they're hoping to hire someone good enough for the

role who can grow into it. On the higher end of the range, they're hoping they can nab someone who's really great for the role, perhaps even over-qualified. A salary range is all about tolerance and risk for the employer, not about market value.

3. If someone asks you what you make and they're not trying to hire you, politely decline. It doesn't matter if it's your mother or your bestie in the cubicle next to you. Comparison is the thief of joy. The chances of someone asking about your salary so they can celebrate how much you make are pretty low. There's really no justifiable reason to share your salary. [Ellis disagrees.]

4. I have no problem asking other people what they make so I have data for myself. When I'm not looking for a job, I have no reason to learn about someone's salary. When I'm looking for a job, then it matters, but I can't have just one data point. I can't say, "I'd like to make $120,000 a year because I know that's what Joe is making." And two points aren't enough. I need a smorgasbord of data points that justify the salary I want. I'm not using the numbers to compare myself to someone else, but rather to help me understand what I want and where I should be.

5. I'm a pretty non-emotional person, but I get caught up in the comparison game when I know what someone else is making. It's only in recent years that I've completely let go of comparison anxiety. But keep in mind: this insight took 37 years of living and 20 years of professional experience. Do you want to go through that? If I can get upset about knowing someone else's salary, so can you.

There is always a way to talk about salary without talking

about salary. You can talk about what you'd like to make. You can talk about what you think you're worth. You can talk about where you'd like to be in five years. But talking about your current salary does no good.

When presented with questions about today's salary, find a way to pivot into: market value, learning the salary range, what you've learned in your research—basically anything other than what you're making today.

But before we go, here's Carmen West's informed take:

> *I come at this from an HR perspective. It doesn't do anyone any good to talk about their compensation with another employee because there are a lot of factors that go into that. Roles are very different. Even if they're all in the same department, one person may have more experience than the other. One may think, "Well, we have the same experience," but do you really know?*
>
> *And there are people who negotiate well and others do not. So, there're so many differences coming in.*
>
> *It is up to the company to ensure equity is handled appropriately. There's always a salary range and people will fall somewhere in that range. Apparent disparity doesn't mean a company or leader implicitly treats an employee improperly. You don't have all the facts going into that decision. There is a range and as long as someone falls in that range, can you be sure something is wrong? Possibly, in terms of how that decision was made, but you have to gather your facts.*
>
> *When employees talk about their salaries*

without understanding the facts, that causes problems for themselves, senior leaders, and the company.

I've been in situations as a compliance officer. When people start talking, it raises a flag and the company needs to address it. They can't just sweep it under a rug and hope it goes away.

It will not go away.

Employees will continue to talk about it and it will spread and before you know it, you have a class action lawsuit because they found the right attorney, they have the paperwork and the data is public anyway. The right thing to do as a leader is look at it. If you're not looking at it regularly as an employer, shame on you. If you don't, it's just going to get bigger and it will come out in a way you don't want.

So, as you can see, there's no shortage of opinions on this contentious issue, but I still stand by my original suggestion. Don't share your salary.

Key Takeaways

1. There's really such little justification for sharing your salary. If you're on the fence, err on the side of caution and keep it to yourself.
2. Sharing your salary is going to either make the other person feel better or feel worse. Unless they're a hiring manager or recruiter, there's a good chance emotion will be involved.
3. Sharing your salary with a future employer is a blessing and a curse. It's best to find out what the salary band is for a role and consider whether you'd fit in it.

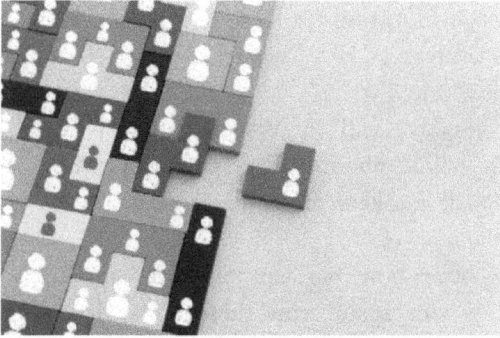

Misconception #50: Your Current or Previous Employer Won't Find out About Your Interview

AS I'VE MENTIONED before, I live in Phoenix. Though it is the fifth biggest city in the U.S., the Phoenix job market isn't that big. Don't get me wrong—there are millions of people who live in the Phoenix area and there's no way I can know even 3% of those people, but the market is smaller than you'd think, even in a major metropolitan area that's growing by 140,000 people per year.

I can't tell you how many times I've gotten calls from peers that go like this: "Hey, did you know so-and-so applied for a job in my department? Do they still work for you? Did you know they were looking?"

And I've made these very same calls to other managers in my network. "You won't believe who just applied for my position."

It might sound catty or gossipy, but it's good information to have as a manager. Clarification: as a good manager who cares about his team.

My network of managers here in Phoenix is pretty extensive. At most of the top 25 technology employers in town, I probably know at least one person well enough to reach out and say, "Hey, what can you tell me about this person you worked with?"

You might recall in Misconception #12 when Tracy Olnhausen talked about Omaha being a pretty small tech market. Small markets mean small networks cover a larger swath of the market.

No matter how big you think the market is, and no matter how unrealistic you think it is that your current employer will find out, there is always a chance that someone will find out about your job application elsewhere. This isn't an issue for many people. But for those of us in higher-level roles, our departure—or even a rumor of our departure—can signal something greater to others at your org. Or your potential new employer's.

"Is he leaving because he knows something I don't?"

"Is she thinking of leaving because of the new leadership?"

"I heard from my buddy that my boss just applied for a job at our competitor. Let's see where *this* goes..."

"Things must be falling apart over there if *she's* applying here."

You never know what other people are thinking about you, your role, or even your employment, tenure, attitude, or anything else. You may not care (or need to). This is something to think about and consider because you might be able to use it to your advantage, or it could put you at risk.

What to Do

If you work for a good manager, you should be able to leverage this network yourself. As much as any manager wants to hang on to good people, there's a basic reality managers have to face: everyone grows and moves on.

I learned from Reid Hoffman's *The Alliance* that one of my first conversations with a new hire needs to begin with,

"Look, you're not going to retire here and neither am I. In fact, statistics for our market suggest you'll be gone in 18-36 months and I may be gone in the next 12. Let's talk about how we can work together to grow each other and get you to your next role. It's my responsibility to help you grow so you're ready for your next job."

I also learned that this type of employer-employee relationship is rare. Not all of us are lucky enough to have managers who want us to excel and succeed in our next role. But, in my experience, most managers are cool with the idea of their employees growing up and moving on. In fact, many managers wish they could take part in their employees' growth. Managers often (not always) get into managerial roles because they love mentorship and sharing their knowledge or experience.

If you know a good manager through the grapevine or from previous work experience, take advantage of that relationship. See if they know the hiring manager(s) for the role(s) in which you're interested. Even if you don't have a great relationship with your current or former manager, it's okay to send a message and say, "Hey, it's been a while. I really hope you're well. I've been thinking about our previous work together and I was hoping you'd be willing to help me out with getting a new job. It looks like you're connected with..." You can take it from there.

If you don't have a good manager and you are trying to escape your current role, expect your hiring manager may find out about your job application or interview. I have been asked by applicants to keep their application quiet and I've respected that wish, but they asked me to. If I wasn't asked, I might not have.

The thing is, you probably won't know if you'll be outed in any way by applying and interviewing for another role. In fact, just assume you are. Perhaps it can be your little secret you can use as leverage later. Or something nefarious, if you're into that kind of thing.

Key Takeaways

1. The world is smaller than we think. It's very possible your next hiring manager knows your current or previous manager.
2. People in similar roles in the same industry have a higher probability of knowing each other and meeting at a networking event.
3. Always be professional, even if things go sour with an employer or hiring manager. You never know if or when you'll bump into them again.

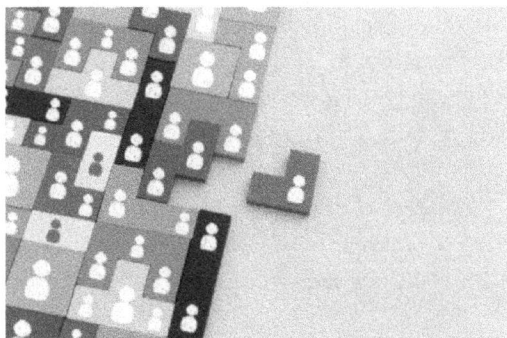

Misconception #51: You'll Never Meet the CEO, Anyway

WHEN I WAS leaving a previous role, I was so frustrated with where the company and my department had gone. In my final days, I received an email invitation to an online exit interview. I spent a lot of time carefully writing about my years with the company. I paid extra attention to not name names, to leave on good terms, take the high road, yada yada. Then I clicked the "Submit" button.

> *500 SERVER ERROR*
> *An internal error has occurred. Please try again.*

My heart was racing and I felt the blood rushing to my ears in rage. I spent, like, two hours working on this exit interview! I clicked the back button. Every field on the interview form was empty. I clicked the forward button to see if it'd re-submit my words.

> *503 SERVICE UNAVAILABLE*
> *Please try again later.*

What. in. the. Ever-living. @#$%?!

That's it. The kid gloves were off. If there's one exit interview response to send, it's going to happen via email because I know email always works.

And out came a wall of text.

> *"The fact that I'm writing this email after a 500 server error on our exit interview is emblematic of where we are as a tech org…"*

> *"The CTO has a nickname around here…"*

> *"I was denied a promotion because of incompetence shown by…"*

> *"We acquired a company that clearly should not have passed due diligence…"*

> *"Our leaders don't lead. They push from behind and tell us to do more with less…"*

Oh, boy did I let them have it. And it felt SOOOO GOOOOOOD.

I mean, I was a worthless peon anyway. Who cares about the departure of some line manager 11 steps removed from the CEO? Tens of thousands of employees and one pointless email from a disgruntled employee. Who cares, right?

The next day, the CEO of my entire division flew to visit me and discuss my email. "Everything you've shared in that email is true. We know you and other key people are leaving because of these issues. How can we get you to stick around to help us fix this?"

I was like, "What? Is this for real?"

He said, "Oh, it's very real. This email went all the way to the CEO. My boss's boss. The international CEO."

gulp

"Yeah, she's giving her whole executive team hell. You're not the first to send an email like this."

I had no idea my wall of text would reach anyone. I figured I was shouting into the void. But I guess that wasn't true. And it turns out that several of the people above me were actual humans who care about their job and the well-being of their people.

When you're frustrated, it's easy to forget this. You're not a worthless peon.

I left the job anyway. The CEO who flew down to meet me ended up getting fired for something I'd probably get sued for if I wrote about. Moving on was the right thing, but my attitude was wrong.

Ellis has Something to Say

As someone who loves to vent her frustration via writing, this sounds like a dream scenario—and a rare one.

What to Do

Setting aside the astronomical compensation gaps between executive management and everyday people like us, it turns out that executive leaders (even at big companies) have hearts, too. It can be easy to be cavalier whether you're getting hired or you're currently employed.

CEOs at companies large and small actually care about their employees. Sure, sometimes they don't know how to express that, but given the choice of letting a good person go or trying to save them, they will often try to figure out how to save the person. As someone who's worked with executives at companies of various sizes, I can tell you that CEOs are often pulled in different directions.

251

There can be days where they're traveling and booked with meetings with fancy people. But even on those days, they can get a phone call saying, "Hey, we need your help. There's a line manager who's really influential in the tech department and he's fed up. He sent a wall of text about his frustration and it aligns pretty well with what we've been discussing internally. What should we do?"

Whether you know it or not, CEOs and other executives may have a hand in your role at a company. You might ask for a salary or benefit that needs executive approval, so they have to formalize that approval. They might get the request and ask, "Wait, what is this about?" Then they're told, "We have a strong candidate for a role and we think they'd be really successful, but they're asking for $10,000 above our salary range." You may never even know this interaction occurred.

I've also conducted interviews with candidates and the CEO or the Chairman of the Board walks into the room to introduce themselves. You wouldn't believe the looks on the candidates faces. "You're the CEO? Why are you introducing yourself to me?"

CEOs are interesting people. They have something different in their DNA. They're often unpredictable. So, before you think about cracking a joke about the C-suite or commenting on what you've heard through the grapevine about the company's management, think twice. It's actually more likely than you think that your feedback can work very quickly up the chain.

You can, of course, use this to your advantage as well.

Ellis has Something to Say

I feel a little called out by this comment. I'm a kvetcher, I'm cynical (if you couldn't tell), and I get really frustrated by leadership (as evidenced by my previous comment about giving a

252

metaphorical hand gesture to a government leader).

As I said above, it would be a dream scenario for someone at the executive level to take my feedback seriously. Heck, it would be a dream scenario if they would listen and tell me why I was wrong, or what I was missing. I feel like Anthony does a bit of that here.

I actually take Anthony's cautionary tale as a reason we should be more vocal. But we should do it in a way that remembers that leaders are people too, and there are a lot of considerations we never even know about. And I promise I'll try to take my own advice.

Key Takeaways

1. Never underestimate your potential impact. You may feel like a tiny, indistinct peon (like I did), but that doesn't mean you can't make enough noise to get executive attention.
2. Be careful with the potential power you hold with your kvetching. It's fine to complain, but keep it professional and relate it to business value.
3. Be yourself and let execs be themselves. They're a rare and strange breed. Just be cool about it and see if you can make something work.

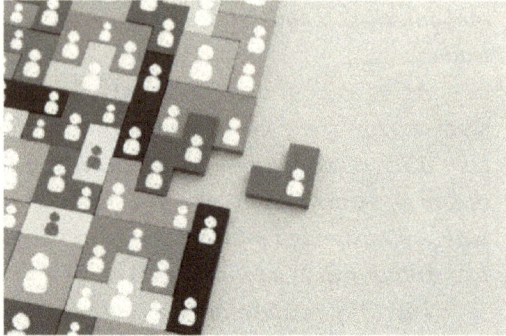

Misconception #52: A Job is a Job is a Job

THERE'S A BIG-OL' difference between being a Front End Developer at Google and being a Front End Developer at Jolly "Fats" Wehawkin Airlines. The title's the same, but that's about it. Not only is there a difference in the salary or benefits (Google's pockets are probably a bit deeper), but there's a heap of intangible differences worth considering.

A few years ago, I was doing some major transformation work at a digital agency. We were grooming and brooming, baby. Identifying talent, investing in them, and sweeping out the people who were least likely to have long-term impact. It was a great exercise to go through as a manager and helped solidify several key relationships that have lasted well beyond my tenure at the company.

As we swept some people out, they were almost happy about leaving.

Some were spiteful.

Whether they were fired or leaving because they were squeezed out, several of them came back weeks or months later asking for their old jobs back. A few of them were even making quite a bit more money in their new roles, but they still were asking if they could return at their old salary.

Why?

Because we weren't providing them with a job. We were giving them a quality of life. Sure, they might have gotten the same job for more money elsewhere, but they weren't actually getting the same job. And in some cases, the additional money wasn't worth the headache, the cost of the commute or the other costs that came with the new job.

One guy I'd promoted from a junior role making $34,000 to a mid-level role making about $60,000 after three years. He left for "the same job" making $87,000 at a local startup.

Turns out, the CEO was in over his head, had no real product experience or leadership skills, and fired a bunch of staff because he didn't know what else to do. He was burning his own cash and his product was going nowhere.

The employee met me for lunch and said, "Look, I'd be happy to come back for $60,000 again. Leaving was a big mistake. And the $27,000 pay difference wasn't worth it. I wasn't seeing my family, I was working around the clock, and I was miserable."

My response, "Man, I wish I could, but I backfilled your role because you were on some key projects that I couldn't let fail."

Don't make this same mistake.

What to Do

It is so, so tempting to take a job with the same title for more money elsewhere.

I had another guy quit literally two weeks after I'd promoted him and given him a $10,000 raise. I said, "Why on earth would you quit right after you were promoted and given a good raise?"

He said, "I promised myself if I had another opportunity, I'd take it." I said, "Dude, I was *giving you that opportunity.*

That's the opportunity you just gave up."

I think he changed jobs three times in the two years after he quit. Brutal.

When you're thinking about getting hired, there's a helluva lot more to consider than salary, benefits and title.

First, the title is almost meaningless, especially at smaller companies. The smaller the company, the more hats you wear. UI Designer at a five-person startup actually means UI Designer/Bookkeeper/Front End Developer/Customer Support and more.

The size of the company and the team you're joining have a huge impact on the number of roles you're going to fill.

There is a pernicious line you'll often see: "Other duties as assigned."

Even a UI Designer at a 50-person company can have multiple roles. It's not until a company has several hundred employees that jobs really align with the job description.

When you're considering taking a job, think beyond the description. Talk to people throughout the company in different roles. "Are you happy here? Do you have a good quality of life working here? How's the commute? Do you feel like management listens to your concerns?" You have *every right* to ask these types of questions before you take a job.

If possible, talk to someone who has the same job title as you're looking to get. Learn about the job. Find out about the day-to-day. See if you can observe or shadow for a couple of hours. There is nothing wrong with protecting yourself from the risk of taking on a $#!tty job. Would you rather find out before you sign the offer or weeks after?

When you need money, it's really easy to believe that money is going to solve your problems. Sometimes it does. I know it did for me when I left one job in particular (I had to pay several hundred dollars per year just to park my car near the office and there was a 10% pre-tax mandatory retirement plan). But sometimes, it doesn't.

You'd be surprised how much a short commute is worth. Sure, you could make $75,000 at the office 15 miles away with a 70-minute commute each way. Or you could make $60,000 at the office that's within walking distance. Which is worth your time and energy?

Do your research. Ultimately, the only person looking out for you is you. The only person who can decide for you is you.

The only person who can identify the right job for you is you.

Key Takeaways

1. There's much more to consider than a salary and a title.
2. Don't take for granted what you already have.
3. If you quit because "the grass is greener," your hiring manager may write about you in a book many years later.

Misconception #53: You Don't Have to Learn about the Company Before You Interview

THE FOLLOWING PHONE call has happened to me wayyyy too many times:

> *[Me]: Hi, this is Anthony from Edify Content calling about your job application.*
> *[Candidate]: Oh great. Can you remind me what job you're talking about?*
> *[Me, trying not to sound annoyed]: It's for the front end developer role. You applied two days ago.*
> *[Candidate]: Riiight, right-right-right. Cool.*
> *[Me]: Excellent. Is now a good time to talk?*
> *[Candidate]: Remind me what you guys do again.*

(Keep in mind, I rarely hire for entry-level positions. The phone call above is one I've repeatedly had for roles with six-figure compensation.)

Thankfully, I usually have a queue of candidates to call. And that's good because I generally don't proceed with people

258

who can't even remember the role for which they applied. It might sound unfair as a hiring manager to reject candidates based on this trivial interaction—and maybe it is—but I want to hire someone who actually cares about the role enough to remember they applied for it.

Why? I don't want to do all the work.

When I call a candidate, I'm not looking to be swept away by the enthralling experience of interviewing. Rather, I want to work *with* the candidate to make sure that the fit is right on both sides of the transaction. I want the job to be right for the human being, and I want to have the right human being to fill the role. It should be a synergistic match.

If I have to drag a candidate through the hiring experience because I can't find anyone better and I'm more interested than they are, that sucks. Not only am I likely to spend hundreds of thousands of dollars on this person over the next couple of years, but I will have to work with this person. I don't know of any thriving relationships where one person wants it way more than the other.

Even worse is when I'm somehow forced to bring one of these detached candidates into the interview cycle and they still haven't learned anything about the company.

> *[Interviewer]: So, tell me why you're interested in this role.*
> *[Candidate]: Well, I'm just looking for a new job. Things are really tanking where I'm at right now.*
> *[Interviewer]: Okay, but is there anything about this role in particular that interests you?*
> *[Candidate]: I mean, I'd like to make more money and get a change in scenery.*
> *[Interviewer]: Is there anything I can answer for you about the role?*

[Candidate]: Tell me what you guys do. What are you selling and how do you make money?
[Interviewer]: Just one moment—I need to ask my manager what I can share with you.
[Candidate]: Cool, cool. No problem.

[Interviewer sends the hiring manager a text message]: Why did you have me interview this person? They have no idea what we do and are just looking for a new job.

It sounds crazy, but this actually happens!

I've been both the interviewer and the hiring manager in this scenario. (In fact, I might have also been the candidate.)

This is truly a waste of everyone's time.

The candidate is not going to get much out of the interview and neither is the interviewer. This situation went from a job interview to a sales pitch. Now the interviewer needs to sell the candidate on the opportunity before meaningful questions can be asked.

Major bummer and there's fault on both the candidate and the person who recruited the candidate.

Ellis has Something to Say

I have been the interviewer in this case. When I ran the blog for a software company, we were hiring a content manager over me. I asked one guy we were interviewing, "What do you think of our blog?"

His reply? "Well, I didn't get to look at it."

The interview was over for me at that moment. There was no way I was going to recommend the guy to our director. If you can't even be bothered to learn what the company does, review the things that fall into the scope of the role you're applying for, and remember it for the time of your interview, what are you even doing?

Always, always do your research and have some meaningful commentary. Make notes. Come ready with questions. Be engaged. Job hunting is exhausting, but the only way to get the search to end is to put in that time.

What to Do

I understand that life is busy and we all have a million things going on, but that's not a good reason to excuse negligence in the job search. If you want to get a job, you need to *make extra time* and effort—even if it means arriving 20 minutes early for an interview just to get 10 minutes alone in your car to read through the hiring company's website.

Furthermore, it's better to reschedule a conversation than embarrass yourself with your own ignorance about the job you supposedly want.

If you get a phone call from a recruiter or hiring manager, there's nothing wrong with saying, "You know what? I know I applied for this position, but I wrote my thoughts down in a notebook and I don't have it in front of me. Could you call me back in an hour so I can get in the right headspace? I'd like to be better prepared for this call."

You can say this even if the notebook doesn't exist. I'd rather tell a white lie (I know Ellis will criticize my dishonesty here) than look like someone who doesn't care enough to remember the job or the company. If it turns out that the role doesn't sound that exciting anyway, that's another situation. In that case, there are two options:

1. Fake it 'til you make it.

2. Say you're not excited about the role, but you're willing to be convinced.

Faking it 'til you make it isn't such a bad approach. It's a popular aphorism because it's a real thing. Humans are funny creatures with powerful brains. We can convince ourselves of nearly anything.

Furthermore, in the words of neuroscientist Antonio Damasio:

> *We are not thinking machines; we are feeling machines that think.*

We are emotional first and logical second. NBC News reported:

> *Smiling can trick your brain into happiness—and boost your health. A smile spurs a powerful chemical reaction in the brain that can make you feel happier.*

There's nothing wrong with pretending to be happy about a job opportunity until you actually are happy about it.

And if you never get happy about it, you don't have to accept the offer if you get it. You owe it to yourself and your potential next employer to try.

If you're not the "fake it 'til you make it" type, there's nothing wrong with a little raw honesty. *A little.* Don't go telling the hiring manager, "I am just dreading the idea of going through the motions and trying to get this job." Instead, say something like, "I'm definitely looking for my next role, but I'm on the fence about this particular position. I'd love to know more about your work culture and how we could be good for each other. Perhaps I could talk to a couple of people on the team before we move further with this process."

Chances are, you'll get some good, honest feedback about the realities of the job prospect and you might make friends along the way.

Ellis has Something to Say

For the record, I have no qualm with Anthony's notebook bit. I think it's a good tip.

Example Questions

Here's a list of questions that might help you know what you need to know before you have a conversation with an employer:

- Describe what the company does in your own words.
- Are they publicly traded?
- Are they on the Fortune 100, 500, 5000?
- How many employees are at the company?
- Are they a product or service company?
- Are the company values listed on the website?
- Is there a company mission statement?
- Is there a Wikipedia page about the company?
- When was the company started and by whom?
- Does the company or its leadership have social media presence?
- What are the names of the products and/or services provided by the company?
- Do you know anyone who's a current or former customer of the company?
- Have they been in the news recently? Was it good or bad news?

- Are there employee reviews on sites like Glassdoor?
- Are you ethically aligned with the company?
- Do they employ any prominent thought leaders?
- What did the company do when it started? Is it doing the same thing now?
- Does the website get updated often?
- Do they have a blog? If so, who's doing the writing? And what are they writing about?
- Is there a company page on LinkedIn?
- What's the average employee tenure?
- Does the company hire a wide range of people?

I could go on and on, but I don't think you need 64 questions to answer before speaking to an employer. Hopefully this gives you a good start.

And it's worth noting that if you can't find this information, you can use this as question fodder in the interview. "I looked for your company values but was unable to find them. Can you share them with me?"

Key Takeaways

1. If you're not prepared to talk about a job application, take the phone call and ask to reschedule.
2. Be enthusiastic about getting a job. Show initiative.
3. Need enthusiasm? Fake it 'til you make it.
4. Can't find enthusiasm? Tell the truth and be open to being convinced.

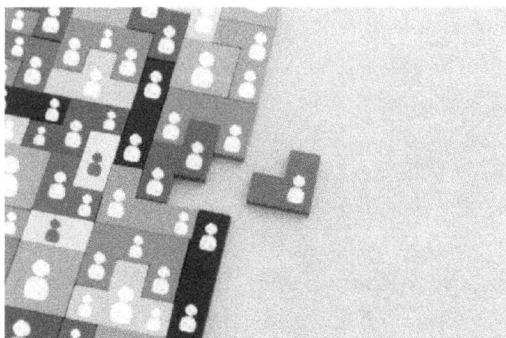

Misconception #54: You Can't Ask For Feedback

IF YOU'VE MADE it this far, you can probably tell a few things:

1. There is no perfect job application.
2. Job applicant selection is largely about timing, coincidence, luck, and whether Mercury is in retrograde.
3. Nailing a job interview is nearly impossible.
4. Getting the right offer straight out of the gate is rare.
5. You never *really* know if the job is going to be what you were promised.
6. Your employer won't *really* know if you're the candidate you promised you'd be.
7. Even if you get the job, there's still time for something to go horribly wrong.

In other words, there's a lot of opportunity for failure, disappointment, disillusionment, low self-esteem and miscommunication. There's also a downside. Ba-dum-ching! (I stole that joke from Hunter S. Thompson.)

But you know what? The moment things go sideways,

your journey need not end, my friend. Even if you get the dreaded form letter thanking you for your time and reassuring you that there were many qualified candidates that made the decision quite difficult to make, it's not too late for one last question: Do you have any feedback for me?

Yes, the dreaded feedback. I can hear your thoughts right now. "Noooo! Why did he have to use the f-word?"

I mean, seriously, when was the last time you were thrilled when someone told you they had feedback for you? Especially at work. Your boss walks in and says, "Hey, can I give you some feedback on that meeting?" Or, you're home with your feet up and your spouse says, "I'd like to give you some feedback on how you loaded the dishwasher."

Feedback is the worst. Right?

Well, it *can* be tough to get feedback. Correction: it can be tough to *receive* feedback. *Getting* feedback is the easy part; everyone wants to tell you what they think. But very few want to hear feedback.

I have some good news and some bad news. The good news is: the further you get in the job application process, the happier an employer is to give you feedback. The bad news is: You never know what they're going to tell you, and you may not like it.

What to Do

Feedback can be the source of much hemming and hawing. On the one hand, you need feedback to get better. No one improves without understanding their mistakes and missed opportunities. That's why people practice to get better at something. Practice offers opportunities for improvement and deepening capabilities.

On the other hand, feedback can be hard to swallow, especially from people who barely know you and are holding your future in their hands. The harshest feedback can come from the person who didn't even ask you a question during an interview, or the person who was nicest to you. Feedback that hits a blind spot will feel the most incorrect.

Feedback is a gift, and it can keep on giving you grief, doubt and heartache. But let me remind you of a proverb that helped me throughout my adult life: A wise person loves correction, but a fool is quick to defend himself.

You won't always get the feedback you expect or hope for. It's possible you won't get feedback at all from a recruiter or hiring manager, but if you do, you need to be prepared for *anything*. Recruiter Allen Plunkett once had a candidate go to a job interview and the candidate dressed up to-the-nines. A full suit, high-end tie, cufflinks, handmade shiny shoes—the works. The dude was dressed to impress.

The company didn't hire him. Why? Allen gave them a call to ask. They told him it was because the way the candidate dressed made him appear boastful and overly proud. Allen had to tell the candidate, "Look, I have some tough feedback that you're probably not going to like. Let me know if you're ready to hear it." The candidate said, "Okay, I think I'm ready."

Allen laid it on him. "They didn't like the way you dressed. You seemed uppity to them because of your suit." The poor guy dressed to impress and ended up upsetting the hiring team. Crazy, right? Worse, Allen says the guy was super humble and not the type to believe he was better than anyone else. He just really wanted that job.

Tough feedback that had nothing to do with the quality of his answers or his personality or his work experience. (See also Misconception #20!) He took the feedback to heart and showed up to his next interview in normal, business-casual attire. He got the job.

Unfair? Yes. Was the feedback a gift? Maybe. Did the candidate take the feedback and do something with it? Obvs.

Here's more direct input from Allen:

When making a request for interview feedback—maybe try something like this and see if you get a reply.

"I appreciate you taking the time to interview me and was sorry to hear that I wasn't selected. Allow me to, first, congratulate you on finding the right person for the role—I know that it can't be easy given how many people had applied and were going through the interview process.

Second, would you be open to sharing what that person brought to the organization that you didn't find with the other candidates you interviewed?"

This way you aren't putting yourself into the spotlight for them to criticize, but are putting yourself in the pool of all of the people who were declined. Oftentimes, I find that this will actually get you what you are looking for—not only a general reply, but a pointed reply.

If you are struggling to get candid feedback—start asking for it in different ways and see if it changes your outcomes.

I've gotten brutal feedback after failing to land a job. I've also given very honest feedback to candidates who were legitimately interested in hearing it. Here are some tactics:

- Ask honestly for feedback. "I'm really curious to hear any feedback you might have had in my application process. Happy to hear the positives and the areas for improvement. If I can't get a job with you, I want to make sure I don't repeat the same mistakes elsewhere."

- Be open to feedback. You may get the feedback and not understand it. You may have to accept the fact that they saw something in you that you simply cannot see. It's not a bad thing. In fact, it could be a life-saver.

- Listen and don't defend. As uncomfortable as the feedback might be, don't interrupt it. Don't defend yourself. What's done is done. They're sharing feedback. The way you handle that feedback could be beneficial for you. If the lead candidate drops out, they might call you back. The way you received feedback might be what makes them call.

- Don't take the feedback as absolute truth. It's what some people saw or believed after meeting you in a weird situation for a short amount of time. The job application process is strange. You have to get past dozens of misconceptions, pretend (at least a little) to be someone you're not, go through hoops and tests and interviews, try to follow conventions that may not yet be clear to you, and hope that you get a piece of paper at the end with a five- or six-figure compensation package.

- Ask your friends, family, and professional contacts to validate the feedback. You can say, "Hey, I got this feedback after I didn't get a job. Could I run it by you and you can tell me whether you think it's worth taking seriously?" Obviously, you should be talking to people you trust who are looking out for your best interests.

- Don't worry about it. Feedback is feedback. It's not the gospel truth about who you are. It's not an indelible mark on your soul, nor is it an albatross to carry for the rest of your career. People change, perspectives aren't accurate, and you might have interviewed on a day where there was bad news. You never know what can influence the feedback you receive.

Asking for feedback can be another advantage you have over other candidates. You don't even have to lose the job opportunity to ask for it, either. On your first phone call with the recruiter or hiring manager, you can ask, "Was there anything you noticed about my resume that could have better explained what you saw? Was there anything that *wasn't there* you would like to see?" It gives you an opportunity to fill in the perceived gaps of why you may not be the right fit for a job.

You can also get immediate feedback during a job interview. According to Carmen West, it's as simple as asking, "Did I answer that question for you?" or "Is that what you were looking for?" It's quick and easy, non-disruptive, and interviewers will often give you an honest answer about their expectations.

Or, don't ask for feedback. It's your life.

Key Takeaways

1. Feedback is a gift. Take it whenever you can get it.
2. Employers are (often) happy to provide feedback.
3. When you get feedback, there's a lot you can do with it.
4. Use openness to feedback as your competitive advantage.

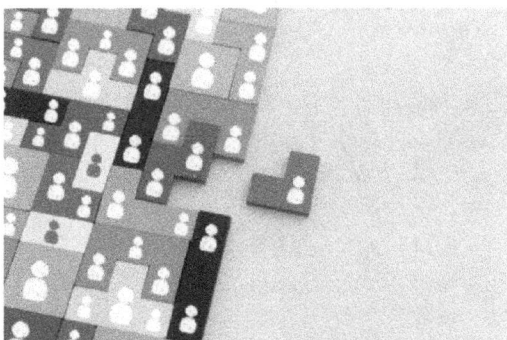

Misconception #55: You Can't Opt out of Ridiculous Interview Processes

IN JUNE 2021, a post by Mike Conley went viral on LinkedIn. In it, he said he pulled out of the hiring process for a job. He wanted the role, the pay was right, the benefits were good, the company had a great mission, and he had already made it through three rounds of interviews.

He pulled out when he was asked to schedule interview rounds 4-9.

You read that right: they were scheduling for interview rounds 4, 5, 6, 7, 8, and 9. This is absurd.

Conley states it plainly:

> *It should not take nine interviews for any role. You have trial periods. If you are still fearful, use contract-to-hire.*

Amen, Mike.

Just because you want a job doesn't mean you are held hostage to the job application process.

In July 2021, I came across a tweet from @urPapaDeyCraze that said:

true story

an employer invited 6 people for an interview by 7:00am, they were all punctual & before the time. he told em to wait.

by 3:00pm, 3 had left
by 6:00pm, he came and met only 2

they got the job

that was the interview
test of PATIENCE

I don't know about you, but I don't got that kind of time to waste. Who knows if there's any truth to this story whatsoever (though it must be true because it says so in the first line), but the replies and quote tweets got it right: this was not a test of patience, but an exploitative test of submission.

Setting the truthiness aside, the moral of these stories is: you don't have to do what employers want. You have a say in the process.

What to Do

Just because the job is perfect doesn't mean the hiring process is. Even the best companies have bad processes. Hiring is hard and they may have been burned before.

I've heard of four-hour interviews. That probably started because one hour wasn't enough and two wasn't enough and they hired someone with a three-hour interview that ended up getting fired so a four-hour interview seemed to hit the mark. Chances are, the company ends up hiring people who are just able to tolerate absurd hiring processes.

I've heard of interview panels with six to 10 people. That

probably started because the two-person panel felt unqualified to hire so they requested a third person and then a fourth person asked to be involved and there were still bad hires so they bumped it to six and then someone in leadership said that anyone who wants to participate should be able to as long as they can fit everyone in the 11-person conference room.

Inc.com has articles titled *15 True Tales of Job Interview Embarrassment* and *15 (More) Hilarious Tales of Job Interview Embarrassment.* Though they're fun to read, they also reflect the absolute dysfunction anyone is likely to experience at major Fortune 100 companies and small mom-and-pop businesses.

Bad hiring processes don't care how big or successful a company is. They still find their way into management.

As long as you're not desperate to take the job, channel your inner 80s hair metal enthusiast and repeat the wise words of Twisted Sister, "I'm not gonna take it. No, I ain't gonna take it. I'm not gonna take it anymore." (Believe it or not, the lyrics to that song are poignant and appropriate to anyone experiencing crappy hiring practices.)

If at any point in the hiring process you become uncomfortable, make it known. You can be truthful and respectful. "Can you help me understand why you require me to go through nine rounds of interviews? This raises red flags as to whether the company tolerates inefficient processes that create diminishing returns."

Or, "Interviewing with eight people is intimidating and I'm concerned it will affect my comfort level in moving forward with you. Can we pare down the interview committee to three people? Or, perhaps I can have shorter conversations with groups of three?"

You do not have to take a Myers-Briggs Type Indicator personality test before you get an offer. But do you want to work at a company that has a rule like that? No, you don't have to take a drug test before you get an offer letter, but if a company requires it, you should find that out up front before you get too far. You don't need to tell them where you plan to be in five years. You don't need to share anything you don't want to. They don't need to know your greatest weakness or anything about your personal life.

At any point, you have the opportunity to speak up, help the company improve and point out where and when they make you uncomfortable. It's good for you and good for them, but remember they have the leverage and can eject you from the process at any time.

There is nothing wrong with opting out of bad processes. I repeat: there is nothing wrong with opting out of bad processes.

Carmen West built talent acquisition processes, teams and systems perspectives. She comes at it in two ways:

> As a leader, I know companies have recruiters and talent acquisition coordinators that do very well, and some that do not. Candidates pick that up very well when recruiters are not focusing on the human components of the process.
>
> There is a real human component. Actions, choices of words, process design, the whole lifecycle—it means something! For those recruiters, HR organizations, and leaders that don't focus on that, that's where they fail.
>
> For the candidate, it's disheartening. I've been in situations where two years ago (before starting my consulting business), I recognized a lot of recruiters have approaches to asking questions that originated in the 1970s and 80s.
>
> Since I have over 20 years of experience, I recognize this path. One time, I had to stop the

*interview and say, "Can we hold for a second?
I'm not comfortable and have the feeling you
haven't read my resume." It was interesting. The
hiring manager was in shock, then I shared with
her that I didn't think the role/company was for
me if this was the style/approach to finding
someone at a senior level.*

*As candidates, we have a level of power. It
doesn't matter if you are applying for an entry
level role or a VP/CEO. We all have a level of
power. You are interviewing them as much as
they are interviewing you. We have to keep that
in mind and understand where our line is.*

*Everyone's line is different. We have to
figure that out and lean into that. It's your life,
not just a paycheck. It's beyond that. It's your
life. It's that happiness journey you're on. We
spend a majority of our lives at work. If we lose
sight of that, we will struggle. I focus a lot on that
for myself, my coachees, and my direct reports.*

Key Takeaways

1. Nobody is perfect, therefore no company is perfect. And
   neither are their hiring practices.
2. You have every right to rescind your job application if you
   don't like the hiring process.
3. Make your discomfort known and work with the employer
   for something better.

Misconception #56: You Didn't Get the Job Because They Don't Like You

IT'S EASY AND understandable to personalize the results of your job search. If they hire you, it's because they like you. If they don't hire you, it's because they don't like you. Right?

Well, it's not so clear-cut.

Being likeable is a good thing, but it's not the only thing. The job application process is really about two things:

1. Demonstrating (or convincing) the employer that you are qualified to do the job as described. When they hire you, they should know that you will be successful in the role.
2. Developing confidence that the employer is a good fit for you and your career goals for the foreseeable future.

Notice there's nothing above about being liked. Liking and being liked are *forms of influence.* You can use your likeability to make the job application process go in a way that's mutually favorable, but your success is not dependent upon likeability.

In other words, if you don't get the job, don't take it personally. It's probably not about you as a human being, but about the fact that someone else made a more convincing case to the employer about their likely success in the role.

You have to remember that bad people get hired all the time. There's a reason Robert Sutton, Professor of Organizational Behavior at Stanford's business school, wrote a book called *The No Asshole Rule*. It's because businesses need to stop hiring assholes.

And all those jerks you've ever worked with—yeah, they got hired because they convinced a hiring manager they were the most qualified candidate for their role.

What to Do

I started the previous section by saying, "It's easy and understandable to personalize the results of your job search." Unfortunately, it's pretty difficult to separate yourself from the results of your job search. In fact, I'd say it's much easier to personalize than it is to detach emotionally from the rejection letter.

You've invested time in the job search. You got dressed up for the interview. You even shook the sweaty dude's hand right after he wiped his nose. You smiled as you introduced yourself. You thanked them all for their time. You sent the follow-up email. They said, "We really enjoyed talking to you."

All that hard work for nothing.

Look, I've had stellar candidates go through the whole hiring process and compete for the same job. Several times it came down to two people. I had to choose one person to fill the one role for which I was hiring. There was a 50% chance I'd hire one and not the other. My team even said, "We are good with either of them. We just need someone in that role ASAP."

I liked both candidates, but chose one. I'm sure it upset the person I didn't choose. But them's the ropes. It's how the cookie crumbles. It's how the world turns. One job, one person, one winner, many losers.

If you lose a job opportunity, don't despair. In fact, don't feel *anything*. Try to think of the job search as a science experiment. You now have one more data point in your job application experience to help assess what you could have done differently (if anything).

It's much easier said than done, of course. I'm not the one paying your bills. I'm not the one watching your bank balance. I'm not the one spending stressful hours searching, customizing, writing emails, making calls and meeting with recruiters. I'm just someone typing a book.

Getting rejected from a job can feel invalidating. I understand. Try to think of it from the perspective of the hiring manager, interview panelists and the employer. Maybe they were more impressed by another candidate. Maybe they thought you lacked a skill not mentioned in the job description that was key to the role. Maybe they had a bias based on who was previously in the role. Maybe they had some other form of unconscious bias.

The key lesson here is that there are probably fifty reasons to choose from as to why they hired someone else, and almost none of them were, "We just didn't like you."

Some consolation from Carmen West:

> *You never know if someone didn't like you, but you got the "no" for some reason. You just don't know. That's okay. I don't expect to be liked by everyone, even though I feel I'm likable. We all want to be liked and want to be likeable, and we all learn that we're not liked by everyone. That's just reality and you have to accept it.*
>
> *Learn to lean into "no." When you can get comfortable with the "no," you're okay when you receive it. You're okay that they didn't like you for whatever reason. Keep moving; it's not the*

role for you. Doors shut for a reason and we may never know that reason.

Key Takeaways

1. Don't personalize the job search.
2. Remember there can be dozens of reasons why you weren't hired.
3. It's very difficult to detach.

Quick Tips Before We Go

THERE'S A LOT more we can say about getting hired, but not every item warrants its own chapter. So, here are quick tips you might find helpful:

- You can build a salary re-negotiation into your offer letter. (I've done this twice.) You can start at $60K and say "based on performance review in six months, discuss an increase to $65K."

- Same goes for a bonus. Even if your company doesn't offer a bonus, you can negotiate one into your offer letter. Use the same tactic as above. "Based on performance review in six months, a bonus of $500 will be paid."

- You can also negotiate on annual bonuses (even if the company has no bonus policy), paid time off, stock options, work from home benefits, and more. Everything is negotiable, but companies are less willing to negotiate for lower-level roles.

- Become friends with HR specialists. Read HR-related books and blogs. Watch HR conference speeches online. You'll get a major edge over the competition.

- If your employer offers training programs like LinkedIn Learning and Pluralsight, use those programs 24/7. You can level up your career with free, high-quality training and get paid for it.

- There are career coaches on the market who specialize in developing people for their future. Consider hiring one.

- Volunteer work absolutely counts as real-world experience. Don't be afraid to highlight unpaid work, even if it's religious.

- Don't bad-mouth previous employers or co-workers. (Maybe I said that in one of the misconceptions already. It's worth saying twice.)

- Ask employers what their typical time to hire is. Someone at the company is tracking it. Find out how long it took to fill the most recent, most similar role. If it took more than two or three months, that's a red flag.

- In the words of recruiter Christine Rogers: "Give employers an experience they won't forget." Make them absolutely *need* to hire you. Even if you're not right for the current role, make them think you could fit another role. Be indispensable.

- When interviewing for a job you *really* want, consider treating yourself to something nice and out of the ordinary. A massage, an expensive coffee, a new outfit—whatever makes you feel good and ready when you walk into the conversation.

- Be patient. Be patient. Be...Patient... Everything is slow when you're looking for a job. "Why haven't they gotten back to me yet?" "They said they want to interview me—when will I get the call?" "I emailed the hiring manager two days ago."

- Always have prepared answers for the typical interview questions: "Why are you applying for this position?" "What excites you about the role?" "Where do you want to be in five years?" Even if you hate the questions, you can nail the answers.

- If you have a spotty work history or you may have skills that aren't exactly up-to-date, consider a functional resume. Google it. It's less about chronology and more about skills.

- Got a professional podcast or been a guest on a work-related podcast? Put it on your resume.

- Interviews are not just for talking. They're for observing team dynamics, how people communicate, office decisions, asking questions, and more. Don't be misled by the word "interview." Yes, you're being interviewed for a job, but it's an overloaded term with much more opportunity than "let me answer your questions."

- There's no book on the market that will get you a new job. That's entirely up to you. The advice you get from us or anyone else is just advice. It is not a guarantee that you'll get a job.

- Plenty of people on Twitter will tell you: "You don't need a résumé and you don't need a cover letter." That may be true *for them*. For much of the world, it isn't. Find out what's true for your industry and the role(s) you're seeking.

- Before you go in for a job interview, look up questions you'll be asked: at that company, for that type of role, in that industry, etc. Someone out there has likely shared the most common questions being asked.

- Step away from the computer. Only in the last few years has the job search become a thing you do behind the screen. Even now, however, networking is still *the best damn way to get a job.* Stop working on your screen tan and meet the people who can influence your success.

- When learning about a company, don't forget to check out the competition. Knowing the competitors in a market can put you one step ahead of other applicants.

- Make sure you have a few people you can count on that will give you a good reference. It's important that they speak authoritatively about you and the role you filled. Don't use a reference who will be unprofessional in any way. Not every employer checks references, but good recruiters will often ask for references and testimonials.

- This book is full of advice I (Anthony) think will be helpful. As you can see, plenty of people (like my co-author) disagree on several points. Remember, I'm offering advice based on what I've seen, heard, and experienced. It is up to you to take what you like and toss what you don't. That may or may not influence your success. Who knows?

Conclusion

Getting a job is difficult, and rightly so. It's one of the biggest life decisions you can make as an adult. Jobs can make or break entire periods of our lives. We spend 20-60 hours a week working. HR administrators use 2,060 hours as the typical number of hours worked in a year. It's a huge amount of time—and a bad job can make for a miserable period of weeks, months, or years. Getting out is easy. Getting in is tough.

Searching, applying and interviewing for a new job is a

full-time job on its own. There's a lot of competition out there. It's a fierce market despite the fact that there are literally millions more jobs available than there are people to fill them.

It can be a disheartening experience for anyone.

Frequently, entry-level positions will require experience that candidates don't get until they get an entry-level position. Senior-level roles can be hard to find because there are too many seniors holding these roles and they aren't quick to move.

It isn't easy even if you do the hard work of getting through all your own misconceptions about getting a job.

The misconceptions in this book are mostly mined from my experiences as a hiring manager and a job candidate. Ask any recruiting professional and they'll have their own list of misconceptions people have about getting hired. Obviously, a lot of it will be anecdotal (like this book), but it's obvious how much misunderstanding there is amongst job candidates. There's probably another eight books that could follow this book, chock full of myths, miscommunications, misunderstandings, misconceptions and other things that start with "mis."

And yet, knowing all these misconceptions about getting a job, I've had a hard time getting a job in the past.

I'm convinced that the right attitude and mindset will take a candidate further than any resume, cover letter or work experience. People with positive attitudes and endless patience are the ones who find a way to thrive. As discouraging as a long job search can get, I encourage you to hang in there. Don't let anything get you down. Bring that positive energy to the job application. Be the candidate they can't ignore.

When you sit down with an employer, be the candidate that makes them say, "How have we never run across this person before?" It might take everything you have inside of you to be that person, but if you can pull that off for just a few interviews, you'll change your future and outlook. As an introvert, I've had to learn how to "flip the switch" and be magnanimous, entertaining, a joke-teller, and more. It's hard work, but it's made a tremendous impact in my life.

The job search is an extraordinarily human endeavor. You elect yourself as a competitor in a race against others you may never meet. You are in a rat race climbing the ladder, fending for yourself, asking for raises and promotions and trying to make friends along the way. It's a strange thing, really, but it's the thing we have.

I'd like to close on one final idea...

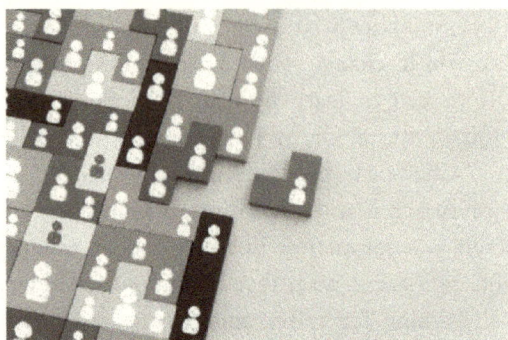

Misconception #57: The Best Job is Working for Someone Else

PERHAPS THIS IS a final misconception, perhaps not. As I write this, we're supposedly coming out of the COVID-19 pandemic. The markets are bullish, real estate is at an all-time high, there are gazillions of jobs, and the government of the state where I live (Arizona) is literally paying people thousands of dollars to get back into the workforce.

Yet through this pandemic, I've had a lot of friends come to new realizations about themselves. They've enjoyed the freedom and independence of working from home, on their own schedule, taking on personal projects instead of commuting and spending more time with their families. My friends are starting to see that having a job has been a crutch.

They're also seeing that the pandemic made them stronger, more independent and even brave. In my network alone, a significant number of people are awakening to the fact that they don't need a full-time job working for someone else in order to make a living. In fact, many of them are starting to believe that working for someone else is no way to live.

I know entrepreneurship is a dirty word for some people and it's definitely not a lifestyle I'd recommend for everyone, but if you have the freedom and the desire, you should consider going all in on yourself. You might find a business partner (like I did with Ellis) and become self-employed. Yes, it's tough—certainly much more difficult than getting a predictable paycheck every two weeks—but I wouldn't trade my newfound freedom for anything.

The one thing that held me back, and holds many of my friends back, is the fear of failure. "What if I can't make enough money?" "How do I generate business?" "What do I do about health insurance?" These are questions answered in hundreds of books and millions of entrepreneurs. It is possible.

I recently came to a decision in my own life: if I want to do something and the only thing stopping me is fear, then I absolutely must do it. If you've been on the fence about betting on yourself, I encourage you to think about this. Is fear the only thing stopping you? When you read the misconceptions in this book, does it remind you of a life you don't want live? Does the idea of working for yourself excite you in every way (once you get past the what-if questions)?

It's possible that you are unemployable—a term I stole from a guy named Mark Baker.[27] It sounds derogatory, but that's only because we live in a world where being unemployed is frowned upon. His argument is that some people just don't have it in their DNA to work for others. They aren't built that way. They have too much desire for freedom, therefore they're unemployable. I'm one of those people and I spent at least six years in denial.

Like I said earlier, the entrepreneur lifestyle is not for everyone. However, there's an intense satisfaction in knowing that I get to keep every dollar I make and when I need money, I have to go out and get it. It's up to me to find the money I need this month. I can't rely on anyone else (except Ellis) for my family's survival. When we need money, we get money.

---

[27] @guruanaerobic on Twitter

We find it. It's available. Somewhere. Most importantly, it's within reach.

When I worked for a digital marketing agency, I personally earned about a third of what we were charging customers for my time. That told me the market would tolerate paying me three times what I was making at the time. The only reason I wasn't making three times more money was because I wanted the comfort of a job, health benefits I didn't have to work for and a salary that came in no matter how well or poorly I performed.

Companies grow because of people like me. Perhaps you're one of those people, too. You help people and teams and companies and revenues grow wherever you go. You make good decisions. People follow your lead. They look to you for expertise, wisdom and discernment. Does this resonate with you? Think about it. Sit with it for a while. Take a few hours and contemplate whether you're unemployable.

You may not need a job. You may need a future of your own creation. But if you still feel like you're not ready for the entrepreneurial lifestyle, here's some commentary from Carmen West:

> *I've met many entrepreneurial types. Sometimes that entrepreneurial passion can be misunderstood. It's true, it's real, it's raw passion. The passion is what drives these people.*

When you're working within an organization, small or large, it's easy to misunderstand the entrepreneurial spirit. Tread lightly when you're that person and know when to turn it up when you need it. Allow that passion to help you maneuver through challenges, barriers, and people in the workplace.

Focus and know when to turn up your listening skills and when to turn up your entrepreneurial skills.

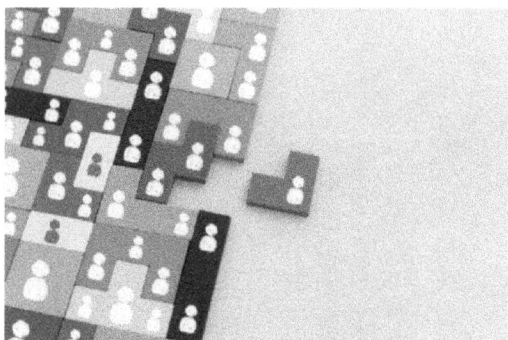

Additional Resources

Naval Ravikant's *How to Get Rich* podcast megasode:
https://nav.al/rich

Resume Creation

Resumake: https://wtfresume.com/
WTFresume.com: https://wtfresume.com/
Reactive Resume: https://rx-resume.web.app/
Byte Vitae: https://cv.bytevitae.com/login
Gitconnected resume builder (geared toward software engineers): https://gitconnected.com/resume-builder
JSON Resume: https://jsonresume.org/getting-started/
Ineedaresume: https://ineedaresu.me/#/

Job Interviews

65 Common Interview Questions and How to Answer Them[28]
105 Questions to Ask an Interviewer[29]

---

[28] https://www.theladders.com/career-advice/65-common-interview-questions-and-how-to-answer-them
[29] https://careersidekick.com/questions-to-ask-the-interviewer/